MW00591191

New Elucidations

Hans Urs von Balthasar

New
Elucidations

Translated by
Sister Mary Theresilde Skerry
Holy Spirit Adoration Sister

Ignatius Press   *San Francisco*

Title of the German original:
Neue Klarstellungen
© 1979 Johannes Verlag, Einsiedeln

Cover by Victoria Hoke Lane

With ecclesiastical approval
© 1986 Ignatius Press, San Francisco
All rights reserved
ISBN 0–89870–041–8
Library of Congress catalogue number 85–82031
Printed in the United States of America

CONTENTS

FOREWORD

From among the host of burning issues, a few themes have been selected. Some lie on the surface of reality, others in the depths of the essential. For some a brief mention had to suffice, while others required longer consideration. No one should assume that together they make up a rounded whole; a number of times they even jostle hard against one another. If Jesus is supposed to "shine through", then how can he be so absent? And if his absence is emphasized, how can we immediately proceed to speak of his presence in the Church—something that many feel is not sufficiently defended? Likewise, some of the things said regarding the states of life in the Church do not agree with each other at first sight. And this is only right. Neither theology nor life in the Church form a comfortably comprehensible system. Wherever God is involved, paradoxes accumulate to challenge the human mind, paradoxes that cannot be reduced to a common denominator by means of subtle dialectical methods. The choice of themes offered here may accentuate the rigidity of the paradoxes; by inserting additional subjects, a deeper harmony could have been indicated. But perhaps it is more stimulating for the reader to build the bridges or to discover the latent existing ones on his own. They must be there, because all the themes revolve closely around the core of the Christian mystery.

ACKNOWLEDGMENTS

Some of these essays have been previously published as follows:

"Does Jesus Shine Through?", *Communio* (1968), 319ff.

"Experience God?", *Communio* (1976), 497ff.

"The Absences of Jesus", *Geist und Leben* (1971), 239ff.

"The Church of Jews and Gentiles—Today", *Communio* (1976), 239ff.

"The Church as the Presence of Christ", broadcast over Bavarian Radio (1978).

"The Mystery of the Eucharist", *Geist und Leben* (1970), 173ff.

"The Worthiness of the Liturgy", *Communio* (1978), 481ff.

"Christian and Non-Christian Meditation", *Christliche Innerlichkeit* (Mariazell, 1975), 47ff.

"Are there Lay People in the Church?", *Communio* 2 (1979).

"A Word on 'Humanae Vitae'", lecture at a symposium in San Francisco (1978), subsequently published in *Christian Married Love* (Ignatius, 1981).

"Obedience in the Light of the Gospel", *Zur Pastoral der geistlichen Berufe* vol. 16 (1978), 17ff.

"Fragments on Suffering and Healing", *Communio* (1977), 193ff.
"Martyrdom and Mission", 85th German Catholic Day (Paderborn: Bonifacius, 1978), 184ff.

"Are There Lay People in the Church?" and "A Note on Lay Theologians" were translated into English by Graham Harrison; "A Word on 'Humanae Vitae' " was translated by Erasmo Leiva-Merikakis. The remaining essays in this book were translated by Sister Mary Theresilde Skerry.

DOES JESUS SHINE THROUGH?

"Everything that can be proved can also be disproved", George Simmel has said, perhaps in jest. With these words, he wanted to indicate deeper forms of knowledge in the sphere of the living and the personal. But this sphere too stands in the midst of the world of facts with which the proofs and their refutation have first of all to contend; for facts themselves always exist within contexts which function one way or another and shed various lights on them.

Jesus of Nazareth likewise—and essentially— exists in a historical context and thus in the melee of proofs and refutations. One cannot object too much when Jaspers counts him, along with Socrates, Buddha and Confucius, among the "norm-setters", although this classification evades the decisive question of Jesus' claim. But did he really make this claim to be the sole Savior sent from God? Former times had no difficulty in their apologetics for him: Jesus worked miracles in order to support his teaching; he fulfilled the prophecies that pointed to him; the men who bear witness to him are truthful; the Church he founded embraces the whole world, geographically as well as qualitatively. Not one of these proofs has remained undisputed. We have analogous miracle stories about contemporaneous heathen thaumaturgists; of the explicit prophecies, only a small number pointed to him, and he himself evidently rejected the titles of Messiah and King for himself; subjectively, the witnesses to Jesus may have been men of good faith, but, it is said, they obviously tinkered with his words and deeds, projected their faith into their portrayal of his figure and finally (John) raised him to heights to which his own words had never strayed. And the spread of his Church is today no more impressive than that of other religions or ideologies. The Church's qualitative catholicity may be evident to the faithful, but viewed from without it is less obvious.

Apparently, apologetics must, on the whole front, disengage itself from the enemy while battling in retreat. The central data upon which the phenomenon of Jesus seemed to rest are contested: above all, the Resurrection. (What actually happened, then, behind the contradictory reports?) And when this falls, naturally the Cross, interpreted in the light of the Resurrection, falls. Then its significance for salvation becomes unknowable, and after it the singular claim made in Jesus' public life, which could readily have been projected back into the events, and so forth.

But is Jesus' effect on history not an incomparable one, so that world history is rightly divided into a time before him and after him? Some would on the whole readily concede this effect, but at the same time underline its ambiguity at least. Martyrs and saints: well and good, but do not other religions, and even forms of atheism, have theirs? And then there are the consequences even into modern times of Constantine's mixing of state and church: the state-appointed bishops, the Inquisition, the Crusades, Galileo, Giordano Bruno's death at the stake, the obscurantism of popes even in the last century, infringements in the area of ecclesial infallibility (such as the erroneous instructions of the Bible Commission). But far more important than all these is the inability to carry out Jesus' fundamental commandment: on the one hand to be in solidarity with the poor and not with the rich (with the result that Marxism apparently had to intervene correctively, in order to show what really should have happened), and on the other hand to give the one proof of his having come, that of being one in him as he and the Father are one. Instead we have wrangling and the disintegration of ecclesial unity, so that any apologetic argument which the Church puts forth in her own defense is in vain. However, we are not inquiring here about the failure of Christians but about the argument in favor of Jesus. Does it still shine through in our day?

It may have been Conzelmann who said that the

Church thrives on the ignorance of the matters with which exegesis deals. Now precisely this ignorance (in part patently willful) is nevertheless a noteworthy phenomenon. It shows that for the majority of the people who are interested in Jesus, the portrait of him which emerges as a unity from the New Testament documents is far more convincing than the subtleties of exegesis, which dissects this unity and produces results that are seldom more than probabilities. And even if now and then these conclusions were to approach certainty, this approach would not prevail against the incontrovertible unified effect of the intact figure of Jesus. It may be that Jesus did not utter this or that saying expressly as recorded; nevertheless, it evidently remains the appropriate interpretation of his attitude. The Christian would say that the Holy Spirit, who inspires the evangelists, gives them the right turn of phrase to express correctly the situation and Jesus' unique reaction within it. This applies even to such momentous words as the self-interpretations of Jesus in John: "I am light, life, truth, the way, the resurrection, food unto eternal life. . . ."

Let us put it another way: does this immense number of simple people who naively find direct access to Jesus, without bothering about the barbed wire of the philologists, perhaps see something which the historical-critical scholars fail to see, precisely *because* they are naive, because their eye is simple (Mt 6:22) and their spirit poor (Mt 5:3)? There is a saying of Jesus of central importance that cannot be excised from the Gospel: "I praise you, Father, Lord of heaven and earth, for hiding these things from the wise and the clever and revealing them to little ones. Yes, Father, for that was your good pleasure" (Mt 11:25–26). Even today these simple people see connections between things which the wise and clever seem to split asunder. How can it be that the disciples, totally bankrupt after the crucifixion, suddenly acquire their spiritual wealth and their unified view of things, if Jesus has not risen and turned everything in their spirit upside down? And if this is so, why doubt the meaning and importance of the Cross?

Why doubt, especially, since here for once a divinity has taken the side of the suffering, the lowly and the wronged? Who will deprive me of such a God who—as an obscure poet in *The Gulag Archipelago* dares to say—had to die not only in order to blot out the sins of humanity but in order to experience their suffering?[1] This is God who not only—at best—from his heaven has compassion on poor creatures but in his Son shares their

[1] Solzhenitsyn, *Der Archipel Gulag* (Zurich, 1977), vol. 3, 109.

pain and helplessness, and even goes further, endowing that pain and helplessness, as dreadful as they may be, with a meaning of love and transformation. Suffering is not explained—but even the Communist, who wants to do away with it, does not explain it, especially not the meaningless, unredeemable suffering of those who are already dead; and the Buddhist, who explains it and offers techniques to escape it, cannot abolish the suffering of his fellow creatures. No, suffering is not explained, but oil and wine are poured into the wounds and there is one who assumes the care of and responsibility for him who has fallen among thieves. "Come to me, all you who labor and are overburdened, and I will give you rest." One who can make such a summons must already be very elevated, and he must have abased himself very much if this is not just a fraudulent bragging. And because both sublimity and abasement evidently meet in such a saying, it shines through to us today as it did then.

But what does "shine through" mean? Surely something more than to be logically certain and thus convincing. The very words of Jesus contain a light that shines into us; and if this is true of the words, it is true above all of him who spoke them.

Here it becomes simply impossible to distinguish between objective and subjective, between apologetic "proofs" that are based on external facts and the so-called inner light of faith that shows us the secret correctness of the facts, words and contexts. The simple eyes of faith do not see the shining truth inwardly in itself, but in the objective gospel, which they encounter in this way or that; but this shining of the truth shines for them, into them, and thus within their very selves. And there is no discrepancy between the one known without and the one who lets himself be known within: he is one and the same.

Today our approaches to his mystery of knowing are different from those of the ancient apologists. We know what it means to encounter a person, especially a loved one. Hundreds have likewise come across this person and know his name, his occupation and his habits, but only I know him from within, as he is. And I recognize him even beneath his neutral words and gestures, which others also perceive and "understand" in their own way, but without seeing the heart. Must one be in love with Jesus, then, in order to encounter him truly? Let us put it more simply: one must believe him and hold as true and possible whatever he says and promises and does; for example, when he calls the Infinite Being "Daddy", as he certainly did, and when he dies, not uttering pious aphorisms, but with a loud cry, as he also certainly did.

Here, to believe does not at all mean to practice

a "theological virtue", but rather to refrain from evading the phenomenon that presents itself, not to wince: on the contrary, to come forward, to let oneself be touched, to stand firm. This is what is decisive. Most people do not face the issue. They have already made up their minds before coming to terms with it. The word "pre-judice" hits the mark here. It applies to great men like Goethe and Nietzsche. The latter possibly did at one time really take a good look, but then passionately looked away; and since he was honest, he always felt tempted to look again. Excuses are so easy to come by: one need only look at the Church instead of at Jesus and one is already excused (who sees the inner Church, that of the saints?).

But the essence of the matter is faith, not a (neutral) looking on or a desire to experience something (for oneself). One who snatches at psychological experiences (presumably perhaps "in the Holy Spirit") will reach into a void. And one who gropes for the flame will get burned by it. Faith is reverent; it allows the light space in which to burn. Still more: it receives from the light the eyes with which it sees the light. *Si comprehendis, non est Deus*: and if you think to have grasped it, you are not one whom God has grasped. Believers, Christians, know the distance necessary in order to establish nearness between the eye and the object of sight, between the Lord and his servant, between the divine-human head and the sinful member. The New Testament is filled with this distance that makes inexpressible nearness possible, this reverence of the Church that lets the hidden radiance of Christ shine in her.

Jesus has no need of apologetics: he shines through. He shines upon everyone who comes into the world (Jn 1:9) and does not deliberately look away. The Church should not pursue any apologetics for herself, but should instead endeavor to make her Lord visible; and since the Church joins the gospel so closely to Jesus, she will succeed in this endeavor only by striving to reach the point where she will herself shine through. This is more difficult because the Church is composed of so many, all of whom are sinners and therefore find it difficult to get along together. But they are gathered together in the name of him who is their light and for the sake of his ever-present mission; so it should not be all too difficult, enlightened and empowered by him, to be in some degree the "light of the world" (Mt 5:14): in other words, to make visible him who wants to form a single light together with those who are his own.

EXPERIENCE GOD?

In real distress, many people nowadays are asking: Can one experience God? For if I do not encounter him in living fashion anywhere in my existence, how can I believe in him? Let us not be too quick to answer such queries by pointing out the limitless ambiguity of the concept "experience" in general and of religious experience in particular. Instead, let us consider that the disintegration of a vigorous Christian tradition in family, community and nation, and the isolation of Christians in a faithless society within a practically atheistic, technical civilization make that cry of distress credible and profoundly worthy of consideration over and above every objection.

What follows cannot, and is not intended to, offer a complete answer, but only a point of departure from which further concrete steps toward a helpful answer are possible. We shall remain in the area of the sources, above all the Bible, from which we shall draw a few lines reaching into the Patristic age. We wish to introduce the whole with a reflection on the relationship in general between God and man, as seen from the viewpoint of a Christian believer.

1. God and Man

God is not just one being among others encoun-
tered in this world and perceived by human senses
and spiritual insight in an ex-perience[1] accumulated
in the course of a lifetime. Hence it is to be
expected from the outset that one cannot experience God as one does a mundane thing or even a
fellow human being. God is essentially our origin,
from which we are sent forth not by a natural
growth, like a branch sprouting from a stem, but
in a sovereign freedom that sends us forth in our
creaturely independence and freedom: certainly
not in order to expose us on a desert island, but
rather so that we may set out on a free search back
to our origin and "in feeling for him, come to find
him. Yet he is not far from any of us" (Acts 17:27).
If we view God and man only as the opposites
Creator and creature, this "feeling" is comparable
to the groping of a blind person who, beyond the
space crammed with finite objects, fumbles around
in infinity trying to find something to touch with
his spiritual hand. Non-Christian religions are just
such a groping into what is no longer finite; in this

---

[1] Ex-per-ience stems from the root *per* = through. Latin:
ex-per-ientia = experience acquired through attempts made.
Greek: *peira* = experience; *peiro* = permeate; *peirao* = attempt,
try, know through experience.

attempt the doubt always remains as to whether the ex-perienced "not" is merely one's own transcendence or one's own creaturely nothingness or really something of God's infinity. Thus non-Christian mysticism always verges on the renunciation of one's own God-given personhood (which is felt to be a barrier) or on atheism, insofar as personhood apparently constitutes a limitation to the divine. But the same non-Christian mysticism can also shift to its opposite: in order to experience God, man descends into the ground of his own being and takes possession of it as though it were something that belonged to him. In such a descent God becomes a function of man who is freeing himself into the Absolute. Such "attempts" and "temptations" will scarcely be wanting where man is a sinner who misuses and perverts his essential drives, namely, his religious drives (Rom 1:18–21).

2. The Bible's Picture of
The God Who Encounters Man

In the sphere of biblical revelation there appears a movement counter to that of searching, transcending man: God on his part wants to encounter mankind. It is very significant that God never reveals himself in answer to man's call or to his desire to experience God. He approaches Abraham with a completely unexpected promise, Moses with a mission that is likewise unforeseen, undesired and stubbornly resisted (even to the point of angering God), and Isaiah, who cries out on seeing his glory, "Woe is me! I am lost" (Is 6:5), also with a disagreeable, troublesome mission. What began in the Old Testament continues in the New Testament, where God encounters in Jesus Christ: he singles out men in order to send them out into the whole world with mandates and corresponding authority. The experience of encounter (we shall see this later) that they undoubtedly undergo is both the starting point and a function of their mission.

And now everything depends on whether their heart is completely open and ready to fulfill the mandate given them. This is revealed in difficult situations in which their faith, their fidelity and their obedience to God must prove themselves. And the Bible of the Old and the New Covenant prefers to attribute these situations to the express will of God. It is not man who is to experience God; rather, God wants to experience and to ascertain (*peirazesthai*) experientially by means of *testing* whether the commissioned person is walking the path indicated by God. Whereas the Bible

23

nowhere speaks of an experience (*peira*) of God on man's part, the theme of God's experience of man by means of testing (*peirasmos*) appears throughout the whole of salvation history: "Remember how he dealt with Abraham [in requiring the sacrifice of Isaac], how he tested Isaac and all that happened to Jacob. . . . For he has not tested us in the crucible as he did them, to search their hearts, nor has he taken revenge on us; but by way of admonition, the Lord chastises those who are close to him", says Judith to the people (Judith 8:26f.). Jesus' mission too had to pass through this testing in order to be tempered in the fire. Had he succumbed to the temptation of a temporal Messianism, he would have reversed the situation: instead of letting himself be tested, he would have tested God and thus committed the same sin as the Israelites "on that day at Massah, when your ancestors tempted me; they put me to the test" (Ps 95:9). Hence Jesus rejects the tempter: "You shall not put the Lord your God to the test" (*peirazein*: Mt 4:7=Dt 6:16).[2]

Withstanding God's testing leads to man's being *approved*. Therefore Paul says he "can boast about our sufferings, knowing that suffering brings patience, and patience brings approval [*dokimē*,

[2] This corresponds to the strict prohibition in Romans against "testing" God's greater grace by sinning: 3:5–8; 6:1, 15.

which Luther translates as 'experience'], and approval brings hope, and this hope is not deceptive . . ." (Rom 5:3–5). This hope is like the light reflected onto man from God's joy over his successful testing, so that James can even say: "My brothers, count it sheer joy when you meet various trials (*peirasmoi*), knowing that the testing of your faith (*dokimion*) makes you patient, but patience too is to have its full effect so that you will become perfect, complete, with nothing missing" (James 1:2f.).

When the word "experience" (*peira*) finally appears in the writings of the Apostolic Fathers, it is to denote God's experience, not man's: "We must undergo the *peira* of the living God and be trained in this life so that we may be crowned in the next" (2 Clem 20:2). But apropos of the reflection of God's joy over man's being proved onto man's own "joy" (as recommended by James), we can now also speak, as though indirectly, of a human experience: "Experience of God occurs precisely by way of afflictions; these afflictions by no means hinder Christian experience and its 'laudatory' assertions, but make them possible."[3]

However, this biblical "experience in reflected

[3] Wilhelm Thüsing, "Neutestamentliche Zugangswege zu einer transzendental-dialogischen Christologie", in K. Rahner and W. Thüsing, *Christologie systematisch und exegetisch*, *Quaestiones Disputatae* 55 (Freiburg im Breslau, 1972): 154.

joy" has one unmistakable characteristic: it is the fruit of a *renunciation* that has been proved by temptation. One can consider the archetypal example of the sacrifice Abraham was required to make of his son, by which he manifested the authenticity, genuineness and integrity of his faith. It earns for him—according to the passage in Romans cited above—a completely new quality of hope in God's promise. At the same time the covenant reality, consisting of mutual fidelity between God and him, is experientially strengthened. Here the renunciation no longer lies, as it does in man's own attempts to experience God, in renouncing one's environment in order to grasp the absolute (in ecstasy or absorption), or in renouncing one's own personhood or God's (as, for example, in Buddhism); rather, it lies in faith itself, which, instead of a self-designed plan of life, accepts a commission from God, a divine piloting in commandments and counsels, and carries out these directives through every temptation from without and within. It can be said with certainty that there is no Christian experience of God that is not the fruit of the conquest of self-will, or at least of the decision to conquer it. And among the manifestations of this self-will one must include every autocratic attempt of man to evoke religious experiences on his own initiative and by means of his own methods and techniques.

26

Precisely this point is demonstrated most forcibly in the Old Testament by the all-pervasive,
tenacious combat of the religion of Yahweh against
the religions of the "false gods". Israel lives in the
Holy Land at close quarters with the Canaanites
and their cults. Later, in the period of the kings,
their political marriages are responsible for the
introduction of the foreign cults of the princesses-
by-marriage. Ezekiel forcefully depicts for us the
presence of the heathen cults—cults which were
almost always associated with fornication—not
only in the sacred shrines on the country's hills but
in the vicinity of the Jerusalem Temple and even
within it: Manassah has erected a statue of Astarte;
the people incense reliefs of mythological "snakes
and repulsive animals"; women sit on the ground
and mourn over the god Tammuz, who died
annually and rose again; others prostrate themselves toward the east in adoration of the sun
(Ezek 8). What we have just presented here in
summary form is found scattered throughout
the entire history of the kings, beginning with
Solomon. In the story of Elijah, four hundred fifty
prophets of Baal appear (1 Kings 18:19). We hear
of hierodules, male and female, who prostitute
themselves to honor the temple deity (Hos 4:8f.,
14, etc.), of child sacrifices to Moloch (2 Kings
16:3, etc.) and other similar adaptations to the
surrounding culture. Without any doubt, in all

these forms of idolatry that are like "a stench in Yahweh's nostrils", the mania for religious experience was much better gratified than in the imageless cult of Israel's God. The prohibition of images did not mean primarily the lifeless stone, as we would consider an Egyptian or Mesopotamian image of a god to be; rather, it denoted a magical sensualization of the divine that was present in its representation. To this process of sensualizing the divine there belong most immediately the sexual celebrations by which a celestial-terrestrial fertility was supposed to be in part symbolized and in part stimulated. The many allegorical speeches which label the chosen people—both of the northern and southern kingdoms—as a harlot, who is time and again unfaithful to her wedded husband and offers herself to every vagabond god, make use of very real occurrences as symbols. From time immemorial, the people was susceptible to this kind of "religious experience", as the memorable episode at Peor during the wandering in the desert shows (Nb 25).

It is highly significant that the true God, referring to the sex cults, lifts them out of the sphere of sensual experience and makes of them a concrete image of the perfect relationship of fidelity between him and the people (Hosea, Jeremiah, Ezekiel). The people must learn to elevate the religious experience that they thought to make in sensual ecstasies to an "imageless", "unex-perienced" sphere, which was completely different but not less demanding existentially. In this sphere, "the knowledge of God", as Hosea understands it, occurs in pure surrender and selfless fidelity. Here the Old Testament prohibition of images retains its timeliness even today: if "image" means what it unequivocally expressed then—the tangible pres-ence of the divine, so that the divine entered secretly or openly into the human sphere of power by virtue of the moment of experience—any cult of images is likewise forbidden to us. This applies even to him who is expressly called "the image of the invisible God" (Col 1:15), Jesus Christ, who always points away from himself to the Father and is present to the world only as the one who has died and returned to the Father. A certain icon cult is frequently on the dangerous borderline beyond which unbiblical, forbidden experience begins. The image of God offered in Jesus Christ must by no means be misused in order to give us sensory experiences of God (the bridal mysticism of the Middle Ages also frequently overstepped the limits in this regard). Rather, it exists in order to trans-form us into *his* image, as Paul repeatedly urges (Rom 8:29; 1 Cor 15:49; 2 Cor 3:18), and thus to mediate to us again the correct "knowledge of God" (Hosea).

To this line of thought we could add still another

Old Testament theme. Major prophecy apparently grew out of originally rather shady phenomena that linked Israel's early prophetic tradition to that of other peoples: on the one hand, ecstasies produced artificially by music and dance; on the other hand, professional prophets who belonged to the staff of a court or a temple. Such a prophetic tradition is for a people another way of experientially assuring itself of God and of his concrete will. But in Israel, something completely different grows out of it: prophecy based on a divine call which, removed from any human grasp, stands in the grip of the living God and at any given time proclaims just what people do not want to hear. This does not at all mean that all the prophets prophesy only disaster; but it does mean that when they announce salvation, *shalom*, this peace is always promised according to God's mind and under the conditions laid down by him and is therefore seldom promised otherwise than as the sequel to and the reverse side of a judgment.

3. Experience of Distance from God?

But there is another Old Testament theme that belongs here and will be echoed significantly by the Church Fathers. It is characteristic of the Old

Testament in a special way, first of all because there is as yet no opening to the life beyond; therefore, the reward promised for fidelity and the punishment threatened for infidelity are realized in this life. Thus the summarizing (Deuteronomic) account of history can describe the destiny of the people in the following very simple schematization: steadfastness in believing—well-being; apostasy to strange gods—tangible punishment, crying out to God in suffering, inner conversion and renewed manifest response on God's part. Here the just person immediately "experiences" his justice in the fact that things go well with him essentially; the horrors in store in the case of apostasy from God are drastically described in long lists (Lev 26:14ff.; Dt 28:15ff.). Everyone knows that this all too simple system, also espoused by Job's friends, shatters on the problem of their suffering friend. And Jesus' cry of godforsakenness at his death makes it more irretrievable than ever.

Nevertheless a persistent theme can be traced through the theology of the Fathers which takes up the Old Testament theme again, having subtly corrected it. It was, no doubt, the parable of the Prodigal Son which occasioned this correction.

Irenaeus is the first to develop the thought broadly and depict it lovingly. God created man free; in his ignorance and inexperience he was bound to fall. He had to make the experience (*pera*) of his finitude and neediness and to feel in his own body the state of distance from God, the famine in a distant land. Only on returning contritely to his Father's house does he come to appreciate what he has in his Father's property. "The harder we have to struggle for a thing, the more valuable it appears to us, and the more valuable, the more beloved."[4] Irenaeus is concerned with man's complete freedom and God's equally complete freedom from violence; God's way is never to force created freedom into doing a thing, but to influence it by gently "persuading" or "suggesting". Hence he allows the evil experience a person makes apart from God to appear less as the effect of a divine punishment than as the inner consequence of the person's own turning away.

Origen's approach is not much different. For him, it is above all God's providence that accompanies the erring ways of free man and knows the right moment to lead him back to God: perhaps this moment has to be postponed so that the person may be better healed, just as a physician might postpone an operation until the abscess is

---

[4] *Adv. Haer.* IV 37, 7.

ripe. "Anyone who has not recognized his own weakness and infirmity as well as divine grace and, even if he be cured, has not gained experience of himself [*heauton pepeiramenos*] and [therefore] does not know himself, will imagine that what was given him by heavenly grace is actually his own accomplishment."[5] Men must, as Irenaeus says, become disgusted with evil in order to be secure in good and, "surfeited by acquaintance with evil and by saturation with the sin for which they yearn, notice the damage and attain [the regained state of salvation] with all the more certainty."[6]

Origen's thought reappears in Basil: Adam, "because of a surfeit [of good], became arrogant", but God allowed him to die "so that the sickness might not become immortal".[7] For Gregory of Nyssa, finally, man's experience of evil must progress to its ultimate limit; but since evil cannot be infinite, his experience must halt at this limit and yield to the process of return to God.[8]

[5] *Peri Archon* III 1, 12.
[6] *On Prayer* II 29, 13.
[7] PG 31, 344 C–D.
[8] PG 44, 204 B–C. Jean Daniélou has an entire chapter on this in: *L'Etre et le temps chez Grégoire de Nysse* (Leyden, 1970), 186–204.

This view is one-sided and not without its dangers. Its backdrop is not the Bible but Platonism, which reckons with an original descent of souls into bodies out of "ennui" with the divine. Here as in the parable of the Prodigal Son, the experience of distance from God is the prerequisite for appreciating regained salvation, but this process can perpetually begin anew. Plotinus expressly says: "Only the experience of evil effects a more precise knowledge of good in beings with insufficient strength to know the exact essence of evil without having been through it."[9]

Maximus the Confessor, constructing the normative synthesis at the close of the Patristic Age, expressly renounces the Platonic-Origenistic view of a kind of necessity for an experiential knowledge of evil in order to remain steadfast in good.[10] Gregory of Nyssa had prepared the way by demonstrating the impossibility of ever feeling surfeited with the vision of the infinite God: every "satiety" with divine truth and beauty opens up new, still unplumbed depths; in eternal life, repose and movement are one. And finally, the convic-

[9] *Enn.* 4, 4, 8; cf. 4, 8, 7. Bréhier thinks of the influence of stoic theodicy and refers to Chrysippus (Arnim, *Stoicorum Vet.* frag. II, nos. 1175, 1152).
[10] Cf. my *Kosmische Liturgie: Das Weltbild Maximus des Bekenners*, 2nd ed. (Einsiedeln: Johannes Verlag, 1961), 124f.

tion prevails that the "experience of evil", that perpetual seduction of the human being that began with the whispering of the serpent in paradise, has no positive result whatever, as Augustine will determine through painful experience; while Thomas Aquinas says of God that he knows evil only as the limit of good, in the same way that he knows all the limits of the creature.[11]

The parable of the Prodigal Son, therefore, is not the sketch of a necessary Christian path; rather, it shows God's love for the erring and includes the two-fold warning against taking a road that leads to distance from God and (for the elder brother) against failing to recognize the grace of God's nearness.

4. Pledge of the Spirit

We have said that the Bible has no word for religious experience, because it is not concerned primarily with man's religious sensibility, but with his docility to the divine self-revelation and to the mission it entails. The person who faithfully and perseveringly carries out this mission is "approved", and on him there falls, as though

[11] C. Gent. I 71.

reflected, something of God's joy in seeing his salvific will accomplished on earth as in heaven. But this is not an event exterior to man: in living faith that includes hope and love, the germ of divine life is implanted in him and grows along with his practical, lived fidelity, assuring him in a mysterious way that he is on the right road to the Father and indeed is his beloved child. The Spirit within us "bears witness to our spirit that we are God's children" (Rom 8:16; cf. Gal 4:6; 1 Jn 5:10). But the passage continues: "We must suffer with him [Christ] in order to be glorified with him." What can in some sense be called an experience of the Spirit[12] cannot for a moment be separated from walking faithfully along the way of Christ. It is an inner certainty given only in the process of treading the path. If one were to stop and reflect on this light in order to assure oneself of it, it would either be extinguished or be transformed into a will-o'-the-wisp. We see this in the Johannine words of Jesus: "If you abide in my word, you will truly be my disciples; you will know the truth [inwardly, essentially] and the truth will make you free" (Jn 8:31).

[12] But one would do better to remain with the figurative biblical term, "pledge" or "guarantee" of the Spirit (2 Cor 1:22; Eph 1:14), for this also indicates the incompleteness of the present gift and shows us the way to the "full payment" in eternal life.

Precisely in this perspective, however, a difficulty appears. Active faith means following Jesus; but Jesus' mission leads him on a course from heaven deeper and deeper into the world of sinners, until finally on the Cross he assumes, in their stead, their experience of distance from God, even of abandonment by God, and thus of the very loss of that lucid security promised to the "proven" faithful. This paradox must be borne; and from the Christian point of view the juxtaposition of temporal moments—of hours, days, years—exists not least for the purpose of rendering possible the sequence of these seemingly incompatible Christian life experiences. Paul experienced and formulated this paradox. He knows two things: that even amid all his sorrows (which can reach the point of "despairing of life") God "comforts" him; and that his, Paul's, "sufferings in Christ" redound to the consolation and inner strengthening of the Church (2 Cor 1:4–7). One can sense the many varied nuances possible here. A person can experience extreme affliction outwardly and at the same time be inwardly "comforted", that is, know that he is living fully within God's will: many martyrs knew this. It can also happen that a person experiences darkness in the depths of his being—is submerged in God's "testing", of which we spoke in the beginning—and in his darkness radiates light to others, though he himself does

not feel or realize it at all. This is surely the case
with many seriously ill people who can no longer
see any meaning in their hopeless suffering, any
more than he who was crucified for us all could see
any meaning in his godforsakenness.

It is God who arranges the "theological states"
of the believer, plunging him at one time into the
deep waters of the Cross where he is not allowed
to experience any consolation, and then into the
grace given by resurrection of a hope which
brings with it the certainty that it does not deceive. No one is able or permitted to fit these
"theological states" into a system that can be
manipulated and surveyed to any extent by man.
Their every aspect, even when they seemingly
contradict one another, is christological and therefore left to God's disposition.

At most, one can say that the states of a Christian
who is being tried usually deepen together. There
will be greater security the more the "gifts of
the Holy Spirit" develop through the practice of
living faith in the individual's life.[13] But one cannot expect this development to take place in linear
fashion—for instance, to result in a normally attainable mystical experience—for to further his

[13] Thomas Aquinas describes this in his famous tract on
the gifts of the Spirit in *Summa Theologica* II–I q. 68; II–II q. 8,
9, 19, 45, 52, 121, 139.

saving plan, God is always free to withdraw special graces from an individual (especially one who is completely surrendered!) in order to give them to other members of the mystical body of Christ.

Hence, in this area, the rules of procedure governing the possible "theological states" in the Christian's spiritual life are discretionary in character, as they grow out of the centuries-old experience of the Church. Though these rules steer clear of any systematizing which would infringe on God's freedom, they operate with a measure of certainty within the sphere in which the following of Christ in the Holy Spirit can take place.

5. Losing and Regaining Balance

The "rules" governing inner experience developed only laboriously in the midst of a continually changing history. Time and again, groups of zealous Christians have succumbed to the temptation to transform "the pledge of the Holy Spirit" in the souls of the faithful into an immediate and verifiable possession.

As early as the second century, Montanus and his prophetesses claimed to be incarnations of the holy, prophetic Spirit, who proclaimed an exaggeratedly rigorous code of ethics through them. The zealot Tertullian joined this sect, letting himself be persuaded by its integralism. Whereas the Montanists had begun by appropriating to themselves the "gift of prophecy", the Euchites (in Syriac, Messalians) in the fifth century took as their point of departure the Pauline injunction to pray always. According to them, neither the Church's sacraments nor mere asceticism were able to overcome the evil ravaging the human soul; only the Holy Spirit dwelling experientially in the soul as a result of prayer could expel it. The writings of this widely ramified, influential movement were in part made to resemble Church orthodoxy (as in the well-known fifty Pseudo-Macarian homilies), and the transitions to genuine Church literature are smooth. In addition, apart from Messalian influence, early monasticism eagerly engaged in reflection on states of prayer and on the presence of the Holy Spirit and of the evil spirit in the soul (Evagrius Ponticus), leading to "discernment of spirits". As a result, the word "experience" (*peira*), endowed with a new and positive meaning, began to play an important role in these circles.

One can observe this in Diadochus, the genial Bishop of Photice, to cite one characteristic example. Though a shrewd opponent of Messalian doctrine, he nevertheless at the same time adopted many points of its concept of experience.[14] He speaks of an "experience of agape", a "spiritual experience", an "experience of faith", an "experience of enlightenment", and so forth. Yet with Diadochus, intensive observations of "theological states" in the soul of the person who prays and is zealously seeking God are completely oriented to a (thoroughly orthodox) teaching on discernment of spirits. Not without reason, his work was recommended reading in the first novitiates of the Society of Jesus.

Maximus the Confessor learns much from Diadochus and assimilates what he learns into his *Maxims of Charity*,[15] and the doctrine of discernment of spirits is transmitted without significant interruption throughout the Middle Ages down to the Ignatian Spiritual Exercises. In every period of the Church's history, including ours, it acquires a new timeliness, especially since the relationship between pure faith and concomitant faith experience cannot be reduced to a simple common denominator.

---

[14] See the texts entered in the index under *"peira"* in the edition by Eduard des Places of *Oeuvres spirituelles*, *Sources chrétiennes*, 5ff. (1955).

[15] These are translated in *Kosmische Liturgie*, 408–81.

6. The Consequences for Today

In the Bible, in both Old and New Testaments, the relationship between God and mankind is described chiefly under the headings of revelation and faith. And it is true that revelation is transmitted through individuals, of whom one can say that as prophets or visionaries they possess a different, more experiential knowledge of God than those who "believe because they hear" (Rom 10:17). It is likewise true that the disciples' eyes and ears are called blessed, because they see and hear what so many others before them have longed to see and hear (Mt 13:16f.). But this beatitude actually receives its force only after Easter, when the Lord disappears from the disciples: during their "contemporaneity" with him they did not yet really see and hear at all.[16] And it is precisely in *this* "seeing and hearing", which becomes actual only in the moment of the Lord's withdrawal ("It is good for you that I go"), that the Apostles' experience becomes archetypal for succeeding generations.[17] On the one hand, the generations to come are de-

---

[16] On this see the excellent exposition of Kierkegaard's concept of "contemporaneity" and its ecclesial correction by Fernand Guimet, *Existenz und Ewigkeit* (Einsiedeln: Johannes Verlag, 1973), 39–49.

[17] On this see my *Herrlichkeit*, 2nd ed. (Einsiedeln: Johannes Verlag, 1968), vol. 1, 290ff.

prived of "seeing and hearing": "Happy are those who have not seen and yet believe" (Jn 20:29; cf. 1 Pet 1:8); on the other hand, they are drawn by faith into the archetypal experience of the eye-witnesses on the same footing with them: "What we have heard, what we have seen with our own eyes and touched with our hands . . . of the Word of life [not 'the historical Jesus']—this is what we bear witness to and proclaim to you . . . so that you too may be in union with us" (1 Jn 1:1–3).

Evidently, according to John's letter, this sharing in the "experience" of the original revelation of Christ, which should explicitly bring about "union", is attainable only if the hearers are drawn into a community of faith which implies a realization of Christ in the Holy Spirit: "I in them", prays Jesus, "and you in me, that they may be completely one, so that the world will know . . ." (Jn 17:23). When Paul speaks of the faith that comes from hearing, he too always has in view the living witness of the proclaimer and, behind him, of the community. This means that in the absence of any experience of Christian reality, no access to faith is possible. In this connection, however, we must understand that this Christian vitality is to be measured against the content of faith—God's deed in the living Christ—and not against the subjective experience of the act of faith.

Here we have again arrived at the *renunciation*

(of immediate experience) which we stressed in the beginning and which constitutes the condition for every truly Christian experience of faith. Perhaps no one has understood and described this point so well as Maurice Blondel.[18] It is only when we renounce every partial experience and every subjective guarantee of possessing what is experienced that we receive totality of being, the divine mystery. God needs selfless vessels into which he can pour his essential selflessness.

The law of renunciation can become very difficult for the individual in times when genuine ecclesial life finds feeble expression and numerous sects offer the enticement of immediate "experiences". But no one who experiences this difficulty should think that the mystic, with his apparently immediate experiences of divine things, has an easier life. For every true mysticism, however rich it may be in visions and other experiences of God, is subject at least as strictly to the law of the Cross—that is, of non-experience—as is the existence of someone apparently forgotten in the desert of secular daily life. Perhaps the mystic has to pass through dry periods that are even more severe. Where this is not the case, where we are offered

[18] Cf. Manuel Ossa B., "Possession de l'être et abnégation dans la philosophie de Maurice Blondel", in *Revue d'ascétique et de mystique* 38 (1962): 483–509.

acquirable techniques to attain a mysticism without bitterness and the humiliations of the Cross, we can be certain that it is not authentically Christian and has no Christian significance.

Let us always keep in mind that the Bible does not use the word "experience" and addresses the fact only indirectly, as one aspect of other more essential subjects: faith as renunciatory surrender of one's self and of one's own knowledge as ultimate norm; being proven by enduring the trials God uses to "experience" whether the believer is faithful to him. The supernatural can in no case be immediately experienced. When the early Church called the sacrament of baptism "illumination" (*illuminatio*), she meant to indicate an objective happening and not a subjectively verifiable one.[19]

When God draws near to us in Jesus Christ, even desiring to dwell in us, it does not mean that he forfeits any of his grandeur and incomprehensibility. Instead, these attributes, which until then were hardly more than abstractions to us, suddenly acquire a splendor that makes them concrete for us at the moment when we realize that we are called and are children of the divine Father.

[19] When Paul speaks of a living penetration into the faith, he uses the word *epignosis*, understanding, and not "experience" (Phil 1:9f., etc.); *aisthesis* (in the same connection) does not mean sense experience but moral understanding, discretion.

THE ABSENCES OF JESUS

For human thought, and still more for human feeling and experience, God's presence and absence in the world are an unsearchable mystery. It would seem that we can think and speak of it solely in dialectical, mutually invalidating statements. This is because when the concept "God" is outlined as its content requires, God is "everything" (*to pân estin autos*: Sir 43:27), since nothing can exist outside God and nothing can be added to him, and he is at the same time "above all his works" (*para panta ta erga autou*: Sir 43:28), for none of these works is God; each is distinct from him by virtue of the infinite distance and contrast between the absolute and the relative. The more God has to be in all things so that they may exist at all, the more he is in them as the one who is completely other than they: the more immanent he is, the more he is transcendent. In itself, this dialectic is correct, but it sounds hollow and is difficult to translate into religious experience.

In human form, the Son has "made known" the Father, whom no one had ever seen (Jn 1:18); as the incarnate Word, he clothed the ineffable in human categories, but in such a way that in all that is comprehensible the essentially incomprehensible

God shines through. Jesus would not have revealed the Father to us as his Word, had he brought us only his immanence and not his transcendence, and indeed simultaneously, in the totality of his life: just as God is at one and the same time in and beyond us, near and far, tangible and elusive. Jesus has to teach us that "in him we see our God made visible and so are caught up in love of the God we cannot see" (Christmas Preface). God is not the point of balance between immanence and transcendence; rather, his total immanence tells us of his ever-greater transcendence. Only in view of his transcendence, his being God in himself, does he immanate to the creature, descending in grace and fidelity and eternal covenant to the almost-nothing that we are. This becomes manifest in the manner in which Jesus' permanent state of being with us is realized by means of increasingly pronounced withdrawals and absences. It would almost seem that his coming into the world was merely the occasion for his disappearance: "Now I leave the world and go to the Father" (Jn 16:28). But this "going to the Father" is the very manner of his returning or remaining. "You heard me say to you: I am going away and shall return to you. If you loved me you would be glad that I am going to the Father" (Jn 14:28). There are two reasons for this. The first is added to the same sentence:

"For the Father is greater than I." In Jesus' disappearing to go to the greater God, he enters into
his own proper form, which was prefigured on
the Mount of the Transfiguration and became
definitive for him at the Resurrection. The disciples must show the genuineness of their love by
allowing him this form in place of that transient,
material one which he had assumed for love of
them and in which they experience him as present.
The other reason is expressed in the statement: "I
am telling you the truth: it is for your good that I
am going, for unless I go, the Paraclete will not
come to you; but if I do go, I will send him to you"
(16:7). This means that this last indicated presence
of God, the Spirit of the Father and of the Son, can
become a reality only in the Son's withdrawal of
his physical presence, and indeed only in its being
accepted. Jesus expects that in this renunciation
their love for him and for his consummation in
God will prevail over what is necessarily painful
for sentient human beings. Without the pain of
this renunciation, spiritual joy cannot be won at
all. Hence the reproof: "But now I am going to
him who sent me, and none of you has asked,
'Where are you going?' Yet because I have told
you this, sadness has filled your hearts" (16:5).
In the Spirit, he really comes back to them; repeatedly his return is expressly promised (Jn 14:3,

21, 23, 28; 16:16; cf. Mt 18:20; 28:20). But as a real presence, it will henceforth be a pneumatic one—which is also true of the Eucharist—and thus a presence which presupposes his sensible absence.

Now, it is certainly not true that the incarnate Son spent most of his time on earth in leave-taking and disappearing. To assert this would be tantamount to making him a pseudo-gnostic phantom that does not really touch the ground and has never truly known the realism of physical existence. Jesus' life is full of immediate, palpable nearness, especially to "tax-collectors and sinners", with whom he is in the habit of dining; to the sick, whose damaged bodies he touches and daubs with saliva; to lepers, on whom he lays his hands; to children, whom he embraces. All the people, and especially the disciples, are so exercised in and accustomed to this intense presence that they must experience the withdrawal, departure and absence as a very express act of Jesus as well as of their own. His departure, announced but not understood, can at first only be misinterpreted: "Where is he going so that we won't find him? Is he going to those dispersed among the Greeks to teach the Greeks?" (Jn 7:35). Or: "Is he going to kill himself, since he says, 'Where I am going, you cannot come'?" (Jn 8:22). The Apostles, too, hear him announce his going, but since they have his earthly presence in mind, they cannot grasp it. They either naively declare their willingness to die with him (that is, their unwillingness to allow the intended separation to take place), as do Thomas (Jn 11:16) and Peter (Mk 14:31; Mt 26:35; Lk 22:33); or they assert their intention to remain with him in any event (Mt 26:33), still thinking they can defend him and prevent his death (Mk 8:32); or they ask where he is going, so that they may go along (Peter: Jn 13:36; Thomas: Jn 14:5); or they ask to see the goal immediately (Philip: Jn 14:8). But for the time being they receive the answer: "Little children, I shall be with you only a little longer. You will look for me, and I am telling you now as I told the Jews: where I am going, you cannot come" (Jn 13:33 = 7:34 = 8:21).

Hence even the distance between Jesus reappearing after the Resurrection and his disciples living on earth does not invalidate this statement: the distance between heaven and earth remains; it becomes explicit in the unrecognizability of the Risen One, in his "strange form" (Lk 24:16; Mk 16:2; Jn 20:11; 21:5) which is transformed only momentarily into the familiar one and in fact always disappears at the very moment in which it is recognized (Lk 24:31; Jn 20:17), leaving an ecclesial mission behind. Ultimately Luke's unique "localized" account of the Ascension only underscores the finality of this inner distance characteristic of the risen Lord's appearances, which have served to exercise the Church in the correct attitude of faith. But even here a special angelic admonition was needed to send those who were longingly gazing after him back to their earthly mission and to postpone the reunion until the end of time (Acts 1:11). On the whole, Jesus' experienced presence is merely the means and point of departure for setting the believing Church in motion on her incalculably long, seemingly lonely journey through time. The last logion of the first conclusion of John's Gospel summarizes all this: "Happy are they who do not see and yet believe" (Jn 20:29).

But this definitive relationship in faith—which is so very obscure to the senses that some of his close associates "doubted" (Mt 28:17) and in more remote circles the rumor arises that the body was stolen (Mt 28:13), or purely improbable reports circulate ("a certain Jesus who had died, whom Paul says is alive": Acts 25:19)—had to be continually practiced throughout Jesus' entire earthly life, so full of partings, separations and withdrawals, both outwardly and inwardly. Not only do the authorities attempt from the very outset to suppress Jesus' existence as unwelcome (Mt 2:16), but even where Jesus' presence is publicly proclaimed he is essentially unrecognized: "There stands among you one whom you do not know"

(Jn 1:26). John the Baptist himself did not know him until the sign appeared (1:31ff.). On the one hand, he is one who cannot "trust himself" (2:24) to his environment; on the other hand, he is one who is "not accepted" and therefore "not known" when he reveals himself (1:11, 10). This strangeness that characterizes his presence makes him seem absent even where he is present: he goes up to the festival "not openly, but as if secretly". "At the festival the Jews were looking for him and asking, 'Where is he?'" (Jn 7:11). Since their expectations fail to correspond to the way in which he wants to manifest himself, communication miscarries. His seemingly impossible presence is veiled in mystery and appears as absence. The disciples' faith is equally insufficient to recognize him as present in the one walking toward them on the water at night: they cry out in terror, because "they thought it was a ghost" (Mk 6:49). This holds true to the end: "I have been with you all this time, and still you do not know me?" (Jn 14:9). The distance caused by unbelief, faintheartedness or timidity (Jn 21:12) is the prelude to the Passion, in which Jesus does not in the first place leave his disciples but rather is abandoned by them: "Look, the time will come, and is already here, for you to be scattered, each going his own way and leaving me alone" (Jn 16:32). "Then all the disciples left him and ran away" (Mt 26:56). Even before the Passion, failure to accept Jesus inwardly can be the reason for his outer withdrawal and his becoming absent. This is the case in Nazareth, where they want to throw him down a cliff: "But he slipped through the crowd and went his way" (Lk 4:30). So too in the final days before the Passion, when he "no longer went about openly among the Jews, but left there for the region near the desert" (Jn 11:54). In Mark these movements of withdrawal begin early. The disciples pursue him when he has disappeared, find him praying and report: "Everyone is looking for you." His answer is: "Let us go elsewhere" (Mk 1:35ff.), for he is essentially the wanderer, the solitary: "Today and tomorrow and the day after, I must be on my way" (Lk 13:33). The same withdrawal becomes necessary when the Jews, misunderstanding his miracle of the loaves, want to make him king: he "withdrew again to the mountain by himself" (Jn 6:15). Here belong likewise the almost numberless mentions of "crossing over" to the "other shore", which are nearly always distancings. And all this happens in the midst of a public life that is not punctuated by contemplative pauses; rather, Jesus stays uninterruptedly among the people, preaching and working miracles.

His presence, misunderstood and not benefitted

from, is as such the time of salvation granted by God, but as a "little while". It is a time that is still going on but is somehow already in the incipient stage of withdrawal. " 'The light will be among you only a little longer. Walk while you have the light, or the darkness will overtake you. . . .' Having said this, Jesus left and went into hiding from them" (Jn 12:35f.). "As long as I am in the world I am the light of the world" (9:5). In John 16:16ff. the expression "little while" becomes a kind of secret key to Jesus' whole way of existence in his earthly life and in his Passion. " 'In a little while you will no longer see me, and then a little while later you will see me again.' At this some of his disciples said to one another, 'What does he mean in telling us: In a little while you will no longer see me, and then a little while later you will see me again?' They kept asking, 'What is this "little while"? We don't know what he is talking about.' " In this key passage two things interpenetrate: the economy of the grace bestowed from above, allowing the invisible to become visible for a short time, and the counter-economy of sin that refuses to see what is shown and drives it away into invisibility and absence.

Where Jesus himself determines his absences, both aspects are inextricably blended, for both actually concur in motivating his absences in their salvific meaning and uniform purpose. These deliberate absences become particularly evident where Jesus chooses some of his disciples to witness certain manifestations of his presence. Hence only Peter, John and James are brought along into the house of Jairus to witness with their own senses the raising of his daughter; only they are led up the high Mount of the Transfiguration to behold Jesus' other-worldly form; only they—accordingly—are allowed in the immediate presence of Jesus as he struggles with the Father's will on the Mount of Olives. In the Church there are some chosen, favored persons who experience presences of Jesus, while others—generally by express disposition—are placed at a distance and experience him as absent to their senses. On the Mount of Olives, places are precisely assigned at varying distances. The betrayer remains infinitely distant; eight disciples are instructed to "sit here while I pray" (Mk 14:32); the three whom we have already mentioned are taken somewhat further and then likewise left: "Stay here and keep awake" (14:34). He himself goes on "a little further", "about a stone's throw away" (Lk 22:41). It is like a "hierarchy of absences". This aspect is a permanent one in the Church: no one on his own can lay claim to any specific perceptible nearness of the Lord, but it is a great thing to persevere, watch and pray at the distance accorded by the Lord, instead of sleeping and culpably letting oneself be submerged in the absence.

The events concerning the women who were close to Jesus lead us still deeper into the mystery of salvific absence. As a whole his mother Mary's life is overshadowed by the sign of the piercing sword (Lk 2:35), which is essentially also a separating sword. The separation becomes harshly manifest in the words of the twelve-year-old: "Did you not know. . . ?" (Lk 2:49), and again at Cana: "Woman, what have I to do with you?" (Jn 2:4); it intensifies in the scene of the rejected visit: "Who are my mother and brothers?" (Mk 3:33); it is consummated on the Cross, when the Son withdraws from his mother and passes her to another: "Woman, there is your son" (Jn 19:26), thus admitting Mary into the same godforsakenness that he himself is experiencing in his separation from the Father. The intimacy of one's share in Jesus' destiny and mission is gauged by the intimacy of one's share in his central salvific experience. Here the degree of inner participation is the degree of the experience of absence.

What is reported only elliptically regarding Mary's lot is developed extensively in the account of the desolation of Mary and Martha of Bethany on their brother's death. Once again the entire

56

scene is set with unmistakable purpose: the sisters are up in Bethany and Jesus down on the Jordan; an urgent message is sent, asking him to come at once; he deliberately delays: "Jesus loved Martha and her sister and Lazarus. Yet after hearing that Lazarus was ill, he stayed where he was for two more days before saying to the disciples, 'Let us go back to Judea. . . . Are there not twelve hours of daytime? . . . For your sake I am glad I was not there, so that you may believe' " (Jn 11:5–15). When he arrives, Lazarus is dead; but this is not as bad as his having left the sisters without news, in the dark night of God's absence. "If only you had been here", exclaims Martha on hastening to meet him (11:21). "Lord, if you had been here", exclaims Mary at his feet (11:32). Twice the account reports that Jesus was "troubled" and he wept (11:33, 35, 38). This can scarcely be over the physical death of Lazarus, for nothing of the kind happens at other raisings from death; it must rather be over the inner anguish of having to share eucharistically in anticipation his godforsakenness on the Cross with the very people whom he especially loves. It goes without saying that we are dealing here with very personal, grace-imposed (if one wishes, "mystical") destinies and not with a diffuse, vague, epochal experience that "God is dead". Such an experience is much more complex and vague than the sharply delineated, expressly ordained experience undergone by those who love. Because they have experienced Jesus' presence they can now truly suffer its negative, his absence.

The experience on Easter morning of the third Mary, the former sinner from Magdala, still deserves a place in this series. In tears, she seeks the vanished corpse in the empty grave. No angelic apparition is able to comfort her in her distress over the emptiness, not even the presence of Jesus in an unfamiliar form. Her whole being is as if concentrated in the single act of searching. "If you have carried him away, tell me where you have put him, and I will go and get him" (Jn 20:15). Her experience of desolation is so intense precisely because she has stood beside the Cross and there experienced what it really cost the Beloved to cast out her seven devils. In this experience she is completely lost to herself and "lives no longer" except "in faith in him who loved me and gave himself for me" (Gal 2:20). This "living away from herself" toward the Beloved has for her the character of a life oriented to one who is dead. Her "excess" of love is final; by the Easter experience—"Mary!" "Rabboni!"—it is merely transformed. *Noli me tangere*: the sudden presence of the living one is not granted for touching and holding, but for letting go; she is given just enough sense experience so that the Lord, withdrawing from her toward the Father, can set her on the way to his brethren. In the kindled spark of experienced presence, empty absence is transformed into fulfilled absence.

Jesus' existence takes the form of appearing in disappearing, of giving himself in intangibility: it is just this that makes him not only the image and likeness of God but also the definitively incarnate Word of the God "who lives in inaccessible light, whom no one has ever seen or can see" (1 Tim 6:16) and whose grace, nonetheless, "has been revealed as salvation for the whole human race" (Titus 2:11). Therefore the Lord never withdraws from someone who is seeking him and is turned to him without communicating to the seeker the blessing and the grace of his presence. The many people whom he dismisses with "Go"—"Go and sin no more", "Go and show yourself", "Go and proclaim the great things God has done for you", and so forth—carry his presence with them into the life to which they are sent back, at times even expressly into the distance that does not allow them to follow him more closely (Lk 8:38). But the path of the Twelve called to follow more closely is like the path of the Marys, a constant exercise in letting go of immediate grasping and possessing. For this reason we may well say that the counsel to "leave everything" (if it is indeed not really a command) is in a very intense, mysterious sense the path of following Christ: together with Jesus, the Christian too becomes absent to the world so that in God he may be more intensely but more intangibly present to it. Christian mission to the world presupposes being dead to the world, not only in the sense of following Jesus' earthly path but in such a manner that the Christian can represent in a permanent way the inconceivable dialectic of God's ever-greater immanence in his ever-greater transcendence.

CHURCH OF JEWS
AND GENTILES—TODAY

None of the major themes dealt with in the New Testament can ever lose any of its timeliness. One realizes this on seeing, for instance, how alive the subject of the relationship between the pre-Easter Jesus and the risen Jesus is. The persistent wrestling of modern exegesis with this theme proves that the gospel cannot be understood and lived except by transcending earthly life in the Cross and Resurrection and, from there, being sent back to the earth on which the mortal Jesus walked. To say this is also to affirm in the same breath that the gospel can only be understood and lived in the always timely transcending of the period of the Old Testament and Judaism into the period of the New Testament and of the Church. This means that the Church, inasmuch as she truly transcends Israel's ancient national religion, is also truly and indifferently a "Church of Jews and Gentiles". Since this process is continual, however, its starting point, the Old Covenant with its promises ("salvation comes from the Jews": Jn 4:22) and the ancient world to which it belongs, cannot simply be invalidated. It remains relevant for the Church, as also for each of her members, who must make the step from the old to the new Adam, from the law to the grace of Christ's gospel, from the truth of the promise (to him) to its fulfillment (in him). This opens up a theme both broad and profound. Paul has dealt with it in his great historico-theological schema in the Letter to the Romans (chapters 9–11). It is not possible to bring out its full significance in a few pages. We can merely attempt to indicate the theological problem in two concise sections and to draw some practical conclusions for our inner-ecclesial situation in a third.

61

These conclusions, however, are not so centrally theological in their bearing as those we will outline first.[1]

I.

Every part of the New Testament shows how difficult the uniting of Jews and Gentiles into a new corporate entity must have seemed to both partners. The Jews were the bearers of a centuries-old election from among the Gentile nations. They had been favored with God's Torah and his prophetic word and with promises according to which Israel—always as a particular people—was destined to become a lodestone around which everything mundane would collect and orient itself. To have to surrender these prerogatives and consider the Gentiles, neither chosen nor schooled by God, as equals in a new, third community amounted, in purely human terms, to

[1] The works of Ferdinand Christian Baurs on primitive Christianity exposed the problem; Döllinger's *Heiddentum und Judentum* (1838) is a milestone. In more recent times, the essay of E. Peterson, *Die Kirche aus Juden und Heiden* (1933), constitutes a signal, and Karl Barth's teaching on election (KG II, 2) is an actual breakthrough. His achievement is comparable to that of Gaston Fessard in *De l'actualité historique*, I–II (DDB, 1959).

62

Christianity's making an unthinkable and therefore unacceptable demand of the Jews. For their part, the Gentiles lived in the freedom of their own concepts of God and their religious ideas which, when radicalized, increasingly tended to become a demythologized and dehistoricized idea of a godhead. Now they were required not only to recognize a certain human being in his concreteness as savior of the cosmos but also to accept his Jewish antecedents as expressly shaped by God, even though this history was just as strange, if not stranger, to their sensibilities as the national history of any other of the peoples about whom they were unconcerned. In the difficulties and tensions between the factions in the Church, the issue at its deepest level went far beyond a few external dietary prescriptions and the like: its essence was the basic, underlying concept of existence on both sides. For the one, this was the particularity of an election by God himself *as* a unique people; consequently, for a Jew, to surrender this particularity had to seem like sheer disavowal of his very being and of God's faithfulness. For the other, it was a universality (embodied in hellenistic popular philosophy as in Roman politics), which apparently would have to return to the shackles from which it had freed itself, by making an absolute (as in myth) of a single salvific figure, and a historical one at that. What a loss for both! What a humiliating exaction for both, to let themselves be robbed of their most precious possession! What a kenosis!

Naturally, a hidden course lay ready for both, prepared in advance by their respective world views. The Jews were to hope in a fulfillment which they could not possibly imagine, one that would open their particularity to the whole world. Their special "law" would make visible a divine power that can burst open every closed form and even bring the dead to life. And the Gentiles would have to realize that by letting their mythical idols (the "false gods" of the Bible) diffuse into abstract universality, they probably lost more than they gained, and that salvation for the concrete, historical human being can originate only in the concrete, historical sphere. Since the Gentiles were more lost, more "godless" (Eph 2:12) than the Jews, they opened their hearts more readily than the latter to the message of grace. At first the Jews were "provoked to jealousy" (Rom 10:19) by this acceptance of foreigners (by God himself!). In this jealousy they doubled their "zeal for God" (Rom 10:2): throughout history down to the present time, having passed up Christ, they have repeatedly advanced often completely secularized

64

messianisms, and they represent today more than ever a spiritual world power and a political entity of great historical force. This comment is merely intended to show that Christianity's source, its Jewish locus of origin, is just as significant nowadays as it ever was and will remain ineradicably so until the end of the world. Inasmuch as the Church—as eschatological entity—is composed of human beings living in time, and the dualism of Jew–Gentile, elect–non-elect belongs to a humanity set within history, Israel will always enjoy precedence of election (and of corresponding structure) on this level, without its having a privileged position in the Church on this account. Although Israel remains the "sacred root" onto which the Gentile branches are grafted and although, in the end, when the full number of the Gentiles have entered the Church, it will be "saved as a whole" (Rom 11:26), the Israel that refuses to pass over into the Church does not belong to her. It is unwilling to regard its structure as a preparation for the fulfillment to be given by God, but instead wants to find this structure again (together with its paradox of a single nation possessing universal validity) in the awaited fulfillment. That is why it must pursue its self-fulfillment in so many secularized forms. It does not want God to open up Judaism from within to humanity in general by allowing his universal Word to become a Jewish human being, because the particularity present in Jesus (and in his Church) is no longer that of a national religion, but of the Son of God in universal human form and, therefore, of the divine Trinity open to all, the summit of universality.

Now the Church's difficult position becomes evident. In herself she has completely surmounted the contrast between Jew and Gentile (Gal 3:28), but the Church's "whence" remains insurmountable: the theological structure of secular history which is perpetually passing over into the eschaton (or rejects this passing over and is nevertheless shaped by it), and which will always include the dichotomy between the knowing and the unknowing, between those *with* tradition and those *without* tradition, between the suspecting and the unsuspecting.

2.

Not only the Church as a community but also the individual within her is stamped by her perpetually relevant origin. Since the community rests on a theological fact (the "holy race") that is not identical with it and is also the eschatological fullness of Christ, who fills all in all (Eph 1:23), it is in spite

66

of everything somehow relativized. The Church has the right and the duty to reproach Israel for its "obduracy". Nevertheless, she must also let Israel, set aside as it is, retain its permanent hope in the Messiah (who will come again) and proclaim this hope, as Peter (Acts 2:17f.) and Paul (Rom 11:25f.) do. Hence, the Church must realize that she is lacking one of her promised parts and therefore has to work out her own salvation "not proudly, but in fear" (Rom 11:20). Cut off from her roots, the Church can never be sufficient unto herself. Although she really exists, she is always likewise *becoming*, and in the same manner as in the time of Christ, that is, by growing together out of the duality of Jews and Gentiles into oneness in Christ.

No one experienced this as terrifyingly and concretely as did Paul, the "Pharisee" called to be the Apostle to the Gentiles. To those subject to the law he became "*like* one subject to the law, though I am no longer subject to the law. To those who are without the law, I was *like* one without the law, though I am not without God's law but am subject to the law of Christ" (1 Cor 9:20f.). Here we see the twofold difficulty of Christian existence. First, the synthesis, the "law of Christ", comprises elements from both sources. The law and lawlessness are both transcended. But Christ remains a very specific norm which, as such, is freedom—the freedom of selfless divine love. What is imposed from without is at the same time what is most intrinsic; nevertheless, what is most intrinsic is not natural to man but is God's gift to him. The difficulty is compounded by the fact that the Christian must live this ideal in such a way that it becomes comprehensible to both sources; that is, he should not appear to the traditionalist as a liberal, nor to the liberal as a traditionalist. He must "become *like* . . . (*quasi*)" both—not by deception but in the truth of love, in a new kenosis, which Paul frequently deals with when he speaks of the attitude of the "strong" in the Church toward the weak (within or outside the Church).

This becomes especially acute in the Church wherever Gentile Christians (always the majority) have to live together in the love of Christ with Jewish Christians (usually only individual converts). Experience shows how difficult it is for the Gentile Christians, despite Paul's warning, not to behave like "*beati possidentes*" and treat the Jew as a sort of intruder; and it is equally difficult for the Jewish Christian not to bring with him into the Church any of his "zeal for God, but not in accordance with knowledge" (Rom 10:2), or especially of his "jealousy" toward an "undiscerning people" (Rom 10:9). We have a reflection of this existential problem in theology, with its incessant tug-of-war between a genuinely Jewish interpretation of Scripture (by Jewish and Judeo-Christian exposition of the original meaning of the Old Testament and of most parts of the New Testament) and a "Greek" interpretation (by the Gentile Christian Church in its continuing meditation on the Scripture text). Any one-sided solution is false and constricting.[2]

3.

No less decidedly than Fascism, Marxism as secularized messianism can show itself to be anti-semitic. From this it becomes obvious that the expression "Jews and Gentiles" does not merely contrast an individual (theologically defined) people to all the other peoples. Rather, over and beyond this, it implies mentalities and attitudes inherent in peoples and in individual hearts. This is all the more evident since the virulence of a certain secularized Judaism, claiming to represent true "positive humanism", can inwardly polarize and

[2] In Gabriel Marcel's theater, the existential problem of this coexistence is perceptible in several places. From this standpoint, it would also be worthwhile to reconsider the problem (undoubtedly developed on a nontheological basis) in George Eliot's last novel, *Daniel Deronda*.

energize all the hollow Gentile humanisms, while conversely the fact of Christianity present in world history throughout millenia makes of the "Gentiles" those who, being enlightened, turn away from this fact. Jewish and Gentile atheism, interpenetrating one another, form a common front. Christ's claim to be the presence in the world of the God of love arouses the Gentile awareness of the divine and raises it to a level of consciousness corresponding to that of Job in the Old Testament. Kafka's great, typically Jewish novels are as well understood by Gentiles as by Jews; Freud's premise too is recognized as being quite to the point and is put into practice by everyone, and so forth.

Thus, as we have said, "Jewish" and "Gentile" become topical factors in the Church as everywhere, and all of us are faced with the challenge of transcending the dichotomy between them. We can limit ourselves to three aspects as examples. All three are calculated to humble the arrogance of anyone who, because he possesses more, treats the less gifted or ungifted contemptuously, and equally to denounce the arrogance of the man without tradition who, in the name of the "newness of Christ", rejects everything from the past as an encumbrance.

The contrast between those who are prepared

and those who, so to speak, stumble onto the faith has always been present in the Church and is so today more than ever. The former enjoy a formation, perhaps simple but deep-seated, through a Christian upbringing and an undisturbed religious education, coupled with some knowledge of the saints and of theology. These are our "Jews". The latter, on the contrary, are completely untouched by any tradition; at some time or other, they come across the phenomenon of Jesus that comes their way out of nowhere. (We recall that in John's Gospel, shortly before Jesus' Passion, a group of Gentiles wanted to meet him: Jn 12:20f.) Then there is Peter's vision on the roof in Joppa in which he sees the new Church under the image of a sheet containing clean and unclean animals. "Jewish" tradition is not only useful; it is even a theological principle. Despite this, the Gentiles also have direct access by sheer grace, without any tradition. On the other hand, Pentecost with its miracle of tongues is a theological principle, which nevertheless does not empower anyone in the Church to get rid of all tradition in order to be freer for immediate inspiration. It would be best for both "Jew" and "Gentile" to admit their mutual neediness and poverty. To be rich in tradition means to be poor in immediacy to the Lord, to be in a position to envy the unencumbered; but the

71

latter's poverty does not satisfy by itself, for he must still ask the "scribe . . . in the kingdom of heaven" to "bring both new and old things out of his storeroom" (Mt 13:52).

A second point: the "Gentile" does not come to the Church without a tradition of his own. Inevitably, he brings his culture along with him. The Fathers of the Church took this very seriously, as did the Jesuit missionaries. Augustine expresses the opinion that even the Gentiles had their prophets. And Henri de Lubac does not hesitate to assert that when a nation is converted, its fore-fathers are also included in the conversion process, since they have made the current process possible. Open as the Church is to universal human values, she will not on that account relativize (as does the philosophy of religions) the values of Old and New Testament salvation history. Within global world history, biblical salvation history is im-bedded as a permanent leaven and continues in the history of the Church; of course, it can be effective as leaven only if it is mixed into the dough of humanity as a whole. In this position the Church presents the appearance of an entity at once de-fined and self-transcending. Who belongs to her? The Christian who expressly confesses to be such, or likewise anyone who comes within the Church's influence and does not join her? Both may be correct, each at his own level,[3] but we have no right to equate the levels: that is God's affair.

In conclusion, we arrive at the general law of Christian community, as Paul repeatedly and variously formulates it. What do wealth and poverty mean in the Church, to Christ and, finally, to God? The answer is: love. Who loves? The person who gives selflessly. But in order to do so, one must have something to give (says the "Jew"). No, one can also simply give oneself (answers the "Gentile"). Both are right, but both viewpoints can entail the danger of pharisaism. Who is strong and who is weak? Anyone who does not cling to (outmoded) traditions is strong outwardly; but he who does not scandalize his neighbor by disregarding traditions is strong inwardly and more deeply. (Here the "Gentile" does not simply have the last word.) "The seemingly weaker members of the body are especially necessary" (1 Cor 12:22). Is this because they represent Christ's weakness better and are closer to him? Is it because without them the strong would consider themselves as normative and be overbearing? Is it because they are more delicate, more unprotected and hence

[3] Here we need not address the question of the "anonymous Christian". The best and clearest answer to this question that I have found is at the end of the foreword to *Mere Christianity* by C. S. Lewis (Fontana Books [Collins], 1974), 11–12.

more surrendered? In any case, they shed light on the dialectic of the "last place" of the gospel—the place of Jesus himself, the place to be sought by anyone who wants to be "the greater". This is something that always remains imponderable, since the top is always and again reverting to the bottom. Thus in the end the relationship between "election" (Jews) and non-election (Gentiles) is reduced to the ultimate Christian formula: it renders possible the wondrous exchange, the *admirabile commercium*.

HUMAN RELIGION AND
THE RELIGION OF JESUS CHRIST

I.

The slow pace at which *the Enlightenment has been received in the modern Church* has been lamented; it has *taken a hundred and fifty or two hundred years* and still does not seem to be really completed. In saying this, we understand inner-ecclesial enlightenment as *the radically new confrontation with and assimilation of* the contemporary self-concept of man, the epochal *new situation, which is also influenced by the most varied sorts of atheism and by doubts about religion's ability to continue in existence at all. This transposition of Christian faith into today's modes of understanding is a task which the Church and her theology have not yet satisfactorily accomplished. Regarding this task, which remains unfinished since the Enlightenment, there is still a great deal to be done.*

If we ask ourselves what the "Enlightenment" actually was, we could briefly answer: the change from a theocentric to an anthropocentric viewpoint; for religion (very clearly since the English deists), this means the change from a positive historical religion to a religion valid for man in general, who is essentially religious. In Germany, *Nathan the Wise* or Kant's *Religion within the Limits of Pure Reason* are milestones in this new era. Such a religion by no means has to repudiate every revelation by God—such revelations can be considered part of the human heritage; but extant positive religions can contain (as *Nathan* forcibly shows) degrees of clarity and consistency, measured on the more or less integral success of humanity. *Everywhere in the world and in history, God's self-communication takes place in the Holy Spirit offered to every human being*, a self-communication *which itself already possesses as such the character of a revelation of truth* and which *finds in Jesus Christ, crucified and risen, only its full historical tangibility*. Positive dogmas, based on history, are *transcendentally* outlined in human nature. Affirming them, man always affirms at least his own being as well. And since the religious human being is essentially seeking union between himself and God, all the world religions and other world views could be *christologies on the search*. The better the Enlightenment understands its own program, the less it will seek this absolute in contingent historical facts rather than in the inner enforcement of the truth in the subject. This also applies to the Church, which wants to make the *transposition of Christian faith into today's modes of understanding* her business. As a necessary consequence, there must ensue a *shift of accent from the objective dignity of truth in itself to recognition of and respect for the dignity of the subjective awareness of truth*.

Thus the central concern of the Enlightenment was to transfer the principle of the universal validity of religious truth from the divine and therefore unique authority of Jesus Christ to the "human" being, with the result that henceforth every form of positive historical religion is reducible, and must more and more become reducible, to a human religion. The principles of truth contained in the individual world views (even including atheism, which nowadays is continually put forward as a form of negative theology that is at least

76

salutarily purifying) are subordinate to this human religion in a manner similar to that in which, for the Fathers of the Church, the same aspects of truth in the heathen religions and in Jewish tradition were subordinate to Jesus Christ. In the religion of the Enlightenment, the truly enlightened person himself is the truth (untruth is its temporary obscurity); in the religion of Jesus Christ, he alone is the truth that exposes the falsehood and the sin of man and atones for them on the Cross. The two models of religious universality are incompatible: Jesus' absolute claim—"No one knows the Father except the Son"—cannot be subordinated to an "intrinsically good" human nature that of itself (despite obscurities, despite Kant's "radical evil") knows the truth and can come to possess it.

In what follows we shall delineate in more detail the two contrary views of universality.

2.

1. In the religion of the Enlightenment, Christ can by all means be the supreme and perhaps unsurpassable form of divine, gracious self-communication, but the same principle that is manifested in him has been manifesting itself ever since humanity came into existence (*Christianity as Old as Creation*: Matthew Tindal, 1730). In the course of

history various interpreters and advocates of God can exist, each of whom unveils an essential aspect of the truth; and these aspects, which in their historically conditioned forms mutually exclude one another, can—and should, especially nowadays in the age of the unified human race—be brought into a higher humanistic synthesis. In order to achieve this, every apparently rigid and "absolute" text need only be read in its "epochal" limitation and what is permanently valid in it freed from the *amalgams* accidentally adhering to it. In this respect one can be broad-minded. Because every human expression of truth is conditioned by historical circumstances considered as true at the particular time while they are no longer considered so today, a formerly valid *statement cannot be qualified as error in its own epochal situation*; whereas today, since the amalgam can no longer be recognized, it must in its union with the amalgam *be qualified as "erroneous". It was not erroneous, but has become erroneous.* Disentangling the permanently true from the time-conditioned amalgams is the task of hermeneutics and exegesis, which have been working more and more ingeniously since the Enlightenment. In the Christian sphere their field is everything historically conditioned; therefore it includes the contents and modes of expression of the Bible, the formulation

78

of dogmas, but also the promulgations of the magisterium: *the rules of biblical hermeneutics, which since the Enlightenment have slowly come into the Church's reflex consciousness and today are expressly or tacitly recognized by the Church's magisterium, must also be regarded and recognized as rules for interpreting the teachings of the later magisterium*. Hence, among other things, it is the task of magisterium, theologians and faithful repeatedly to test the individual formulations against a *global and original faith-understanding, to reach back behind an individual statement* to the intended meaning. But how is this to happen? Could it be achieved if, for example, the magisterium would, as is desired, *not merely rely upon its formal authority, but also itself demonstrate this reaching back to the original center of faith*? To do this, though, it must assent to the conclusions of contemporary theology, to which exegesis essentially belongs. Let us assume that according to this theology Mary's virginity would have to refer only to the moment of her conceiving (not to her giving birth and to her subsequent life) and that exegesis would suggest to us that the brothers and sisters are "without prejudice" to be understood as Jesus' siblings, thus making Mary a happy mother within the family circle of her numerous children. Would we then have moved closer to the *global and original*? (In any event, the entire parallel

Mary–Church, recognized since the second century, would disintegrate as a deceptive *amalgam*.) In that case, however, who or what would be the subject of this "original faith-understanding"? Not Scripture, since its interpretation is concerned; not the magisterium, which expresses itself in "statements"; least of all exegesis, which has no inhibitions about questioning the understanding of the primitive Church; nor the simple believer, who thinks he may rely on the magisterium for an authentic interpretation. Perhaps, then, there is no "behind" at all, but only an "in"? If one were to ask whether *eliminating such amalgams would not in the long run lead to there being nothing of the "really" intended meaning left over at all*, one could always answer that *a religious assertion ultimately points to the inexpressible mystery which we call God*; that behind every utterance, including those of Christ and of Scripture, stands the unutterable.

2. This probably becomes clearest where we have to excise important *amalgams* from the Christology of Holy Scripture; for instance, the view that Jesus, in our stead, died for our sins (which is *in the last analysis unthinkable*), or that his godforsakenness on the Cross was of any significance in this regard. Since *all true salvation can be thought of as happening only in the exercise of the individual's own freedom* (the word "self-redemption" is al-

together meaningful), and since on the other hand *God cannot be made to change his mind*, the Cross can be nothing other than the supreme *quasi-sacramental sign* that God has always been reconciled. Consequently, any talk about God's anger and all the biblical *threats* (as the proponents of "scapegoat mechanism theology" also show us) can have at the most a pedagogical-admonitory meaning. Hence, certainly *not everything that Pelagius and Julian of Eclanum had to say against the apparently completely victorious Augustine was false*.

Not only the "late" (Pauline) strata of Christology are to be de-amalgamized, however, but likewise central attitudes of Christ himself: for example, *the proximate expectations of the historical pre-Easter Jesus*, which need *not* be *qualified as erroneous* only if Jesus is regarded *in his own epochal situation*. He was simply situated in his apocalyptic ambient, which as a whole—with its depreciation of the world as a transitory, evil age and with its apocalyptic beasts—we are plainly unable to reproduce anymore. It is not God alone who has always been good and reconciled; the world and humanity too (especially when history is viewed in a Teilhardian evolutive light) are at least essentially on the way to the good. In all the world views and schemes of meaning, everything is growing concentrically toward the one anthropological-christological truth (the two aspects of which are inseparable).

The new dialogue between Christians and Jews (in which Christians often enough relinquish New Testament statements as "anti-semitic") clearly shows that Christ's Cross need no longer be a separating hindrance to this dialogue; all the less, then (with a view to the future), should the alleged "Church-dividing" "dogmas" of the various Christian confessions. What will (we are shifting for a moment into the sphere of fiction) already foreseeable ecumenical councils not be able to accomplish here, *"in view of the apertura, possibly the most significant historical event of our century, when the interpenetration between Christian and Buddhist faiths is on the verge of reality"* (Brian Moore, *Catholics* [Penguin, 1972], 39), not to mention the confluence of Catholicism and communism (as in "liberation theology")? Then a world religion would be in sight.

3.

In the face of all this, does a religion that takes Jesus' words—that he is *the* truth, *the* way, *the* life—literally, without de-amalgamizing, still have a chance? Maybe only as a small minority, and—who knows?—perhaps only as a small minority in the Church(es). Such a minority would hold fast to what Chalcedon, paradoxically but without mental reservations, meant: this one, this "who", is God as well as man. He alone knows the Father; he alone reveals the salvation-historical but eternally inner-divine relationship between Father, Son and Spirit. And he does it precisely today, when all other idols and concepts of God pale or at best feed on indirect radiations of the Christian belief in God. He alone can say, "Before Abraham was, I am" (which in its present sense answers *the question in what more precise sense we are to think of a pre-existence of the Logos present for us in Jesus*). He alone—and here the Pauline scandal of God's foolishness in the eyes of Jews and Gentiles takes its full effect—is, as long as world history lasts, the "slain Lamb" that "takes away the sins of the world". This premise (too briefly stated) is the reason why the Eucharist is more than a memorial meal; it is the presence of the person and event of the offered Offerer, as the Letter to the Hebrews describes him for us, without any need to de-amalgamize the terminology of sacrifice (which so explicitly attests to the preeminence of this unique sacrifice over all previous ones).

In this case, the alleged *"late"* New Testament theologies (up to John) would have brought to light the essential, which is of course evidently already contained in Paul and the Synoptics. And Jesus' "proximate expectations" would be completely justified, because in his Cross and Resurrection he would indeed have overtaken and included the end of the world and the sin of all time to come. And John's Apocalypse (which merely completes the synoptic apocalypses) would likewise be in the right, because it was God's boundless love manifest in Christ that first exposed the boundlessness of man's No and the real atheism that does not want to be obliged to anything or to anyone, but rather wants to create man itself. "Had I not come and spoken to them they would be without sin. Now, however, they have no excuse for their sin. . . . They have seen and have hated both me and my Father" (Jn 15:22f.). The term "sin" acquires its full weight in the New Testament, and increasing weight as the interpretation of the actual Christ-event progresses throughout history. Not until a person meditates on the Cross can he assess the abyss of his perdition. *"Nondum considerasti quanti ponderis sit peccatum"*, says the much-reviled Anselm in his teaching on redemption. Because man's perdition is revealed simultaneously with his redemption, there is no discernible way of incorporating the religion of the Cross and Resurrection into a human religion as a single aspect thereof.

84

In every human religion, of course, there lie approaches to an intimate relationship to God, since the non-divine creature can understand and reflect on himself essentially only as a deficient "image" of the Absolute, longingly calling out to its original. God's saving acts in history are not "transcendentally" (hence "known" but not "in consciousness") etched into this longing, however—even if it had always been under the guidance of grace ("supernatural existential")—in such a way that man, on witnessing God's mighty deeds, for example Jesus' Resurrection, would not be impelled to wonder and adore, but could say to himself; after all, on the basis of my own constitution, I have actually been expecting this all along. In trying to satisfy his yearning precipitously and on his own initiative, what he represents as religious objectifications is, according to the testimony of the Bible, not an approach to the image that God has set up of himself, but rather its miscarriage and perversion: an "idol", a "false god".

There is only one who is an unfalsified image, and then only when he is accepted as the one whom he presents himself to be and as the one who is believed in and proclaimed by the believing community. Only then does he manifest the much-extolled love (abused and rendered innocuous in the extolling) of the divine Heart unto its very depths. As image, he alone is also archetype: "Anyone who sees me sees the Father." Of himself, he has the power to shed light.

As Christians we are not called on to build a flimsy (transcendental) framework of Christianity over humanity, in order to use it as a bridge from which to set out on our mission work; it is sufficient to confront the always partial and defective projections of humanity, which is trying to construct its own self-fulfillment, with God's complete project called Jesus Christ. What never occurred to Indian wisdom in all its sublimity—to gather up the dying from the streets of Calcutta —has been accomplished by the foolishness of Mother Teresa, who has thus "enlightened" all the holy gurus as to how and why Christianity is a human religion.[1]

---

[1] The quotations in italics come for the most part from the article "Dogmen- und Theologiegeschichte—gestern und morgen", by Karl Rahner, in *Zeitschrift für katholische Theologie* 99 (1977): 1–24 (also in *Schriften*, vol. 13 [1978]); a few words were taken from his *Grundkurs des Glaubens* as well as from *Schriften*, vol. 12 (1975), 251–82. I do not by any means claim to have presented (or "exposed") Rahner's central intention here; it is evident that as a Catholic theologian his thought is more subtle and differentiated. But despite all the retardant insertions, formal basic structures still emerge. Thus it seemed beneficial to single out certain statements—

after digging them out of their thick protective packing—in order to show that by their own dynamics they "lead where you do not want to go", namely, towards a "transcendent unity of religions", as the newly edited work of Fritjof Schuon is entitled. Regarding this, Schuon says: "This transcendental unity is to be effected purely spiritually, without betraying any individual form. The contrasting elements of these forms no more impair the one, universal unity than the contrast between the colors hinders the transmission of the one, colorless light." The eminent American theologian, David Tracy, S.J., is likewise on the road to such a universal religion in *Blessed Rage for Order: The New Pluralism in Theology* (New York: Seabury, 1975).

THE CHURCH AS
THE PRESENCE OF CHRIST

Let us begin with a naive mental experiment in which we enter into Jesus' thoughts while he was still among his disciples and foresaw his impending death. He had not come into the world for a few privileged people only; he came no less for the generations to come. These were not to retain a mere faded remembrance of him, as of a figure steadily slipping away in the twilight of the past.

He wanted to be a living presence to them, even more living, if possible, than he now was to those around him, who understood his ultimate intentions so little. He could leave them testamentary words to take with them on their way: "Love one another, as I have loved you"; "Let the greatest among you become as the least", and so on. But how long would the remembrance of such recommendations remain alive among them? Human frailty would soon win out over his divine instructions, which go against the grain of the human—all too human—element and obscure his presence.

He could do more: he could let his inmost Spirit flow into them, so that they might finally understand, after his death, who he was and what he had done. And he knew that, to achieve this, he would have to breathe out his Spirit in dying, so that from beyond death he might breathe it intimately into them and send it upon them in fiery tongues. Hence he says to them: "It is for your good that I am going, for unless I go, the Counsellor [the Spirit] will not come to you; but if I do go, I will send him to you"; "He will take what is mine and announce it to you."

But will this suffice throughout all the ages? Will this divine Spirit not become too divinely spiritual, as it were, not only to afford those who come later, much later, a lively remembrance of him who once was, but also to permit him to remain present in person? And besides, his disciples are few, and after his Resurrection he will scatter them to the four winds: "Go and teach all peoples." How can he dare to add: "Behold, I am with you always, to the end of time"?

Therefore something more is needed, something humanly tangible that would guarantee the immediacy of his presence. It would have to manifest this presence and at the same time protect it from man's clutches and from any distortion: it would be a covering or vessel that would contain him without ever being mistaken for him, something that would make him present for those who believe in and love him without anyone's being able to gain control of him by magic or violate his divine freedom. It would have to be something permanent and perennially timely, so constituted that, as a whole, it would point to his own perennially timely presence, his loving self-giving to each man, his personal summons to each man, his availability to each man.

The only means of realizing this was what we call "institution". In his institution of the Eucharist, we see what "institution" originally meant to Jesus: "This is my Body, my Blood poured out for you; *do this* in memory of me."

He gives himself more concretely than we can imagine and seals the gift into a form that keeps it alive for all time to come. And the Eucharist is only the inmost core of the whole institution that we call the Church of Christ. Many other equally essential elements also belong to her which, seen in isolation, could appear to be merely superficial, alienating or fossilized. But evaluated in the light of Jesus' intention, they render possible and transmit his immediate presence. Among these are, above all, Church authority, Scripture, tradition and also ecclesial law, things that people are accustomed to designating philosophically, with Hegel, as "objective spirit", but which from the Christian viewpoint are always only modes of Christ's presence.

First of all, the authority of office: it is an authority, imparted by Jesus, to teach, to consecrate and to shepherd, which (thank God) is ultimately independent of the worthiness or unworthiness of the one who exercises it. If—as the Montanists, the Messalians, the Donatists, the Spiritualists, and many contemporary Pentecostals hold—only a man who has the Holy Spirit were able to bestow it, and then only in the measure that he himself has the Spirit, Jesus' presence would be dependent on the person's degree of holiness, and we would have no certainty at all that this presence was being transmitted to us pure and intact. How could an allegedly Spirit-filled human being claim the authority to forgive me my sins in the name of the crucified Lord, if he himself had not officially been given this authority, with the result that what happened on the Cross—God's reconciling the world to himself in Christ crucified—becomes a reality for me here and now?

This means that the priest does not only point out to me something that is perennially true (I could do that for myself) but that by virtue of his office the matter becomes present for me: just as present as, through the priestly office, the eucharistic presence of Jesus, "with divinity and humanity, with body and soul, with flesh and blood", becomes present for the community of the faithful. The believer knows very well that he cannot effect Jesus' sacramental presence himself—for what we have said holds good not only for confession and the Eucharist but for all the sacraments of the Church. A cookbook recipe may say, "Take . . .", but in the Church one does not take for oneself, one is given. This is true also and especially of the priest. No one takes the office for himself; it is bestowed on him, so that he himself may possess the authority to bestow. The office implies a "Hands off!": it is the Lord alone who gives himself and, since office exists, gives himself infallibly.

To the office belongs the objectified word of and about Christ: *Holy Scripture*. The written characters and even the idea of a book are a form of institution based on many conventions: regarding the meaning of the letters, of the words, of the sentences in one language and in several, regarding printing, distribution, preservation in libraries and so on. The absolutely unique word of God enters into this institution so that, unfalsified and unchanging, it may be accessible to all. Naturally, this is inextricably joined to the free blowing of the Spirit, who is always interpreting the words anew and making them sprout, like a ripening field of grain, in endless variety and profusion for each hearer and reader.

"My words are spirit and life", says the Lord, and this remains eternally true. But in order for it to remain true, Scripture as institution must endure, inflexible and invariable, throughout all ages, throughout all exegeses that come and go: "Heaven and earth will pass away, but my words will not pass away." Paul may speak of the tablets of the heart on which he writes his letter, in contrast to the stone tablets of Moses; nevertheless, he had to write on parchment so that his words could touch not only the hearts of the Corinthians but ours even today. And when John says in his Third Letter, "I had much to write you, but I do not want to write to you with pen and ink; for I hope to see you soon, and we shall speak face to face", he wrote this sentence with pen and ink. This was for our consolation, that we in our day also might realize that there are many things in the Church—in conversation among the faithful, in man's prayer to God—that need not and perhaps ought not to be written down because they are too personal and intimate, and that this privacy is permitted and right because the institution of Holy Scripture allows and guarantees it to us.

But as directly as Scripture makes present for us the word of and about Jesus, it is itself also transmitted by the institution of the primitive Church, by the various *traditions* about Jesus that came down to the evangelists and bound them to something pre-formed, before their words in turn generated tradition within their communities and finally fused into the great, permanent form of the canon of the New Testament, joined to the already extant canon of the Old Testament. At first sight, one might think that this fluid element of tradition in which Scripture originates, in order to exert an influence on tradition in turn, was the opposite of an institution. This, however, is not the case. Those of our contemporaries who complain about the constricting corset of Church tradition and yearn for direct access to the original phenomenon of Jesus, for a so-called contemporaneity with him, know this well enough. But does this contemporaneity exist, since the truth is that those who were associated with Jesus on earth understood him scarcely or not at all, and the meaning of his life, words and deeds dawned on them only later in the light of the Resurrection and Pentecost? Or since Paul, his most profound interpreter, was not a contemporary of his at all, but rather relied on Church tradition in order to interpret him authentically? And in a certain manner, this authentic interpretation continues throughout the Church's history: in the face of deviations and blunders, time and again the magisterium, itself looking to Scripture and tradition, has had to present and define the true meaning of Christ's revelation, thus making its source present anew wherever a historical current tended to deviate from it. This holds not only for the solemn definitions of councils and popes; it is true analogously of the endless exertions of theologians and of saints who, in their life and preaching and in their writings, have worked for the correct under-

94

standing of the original event, thus contributing their share to tradition. This would seem to be a dangerous accumulation of rind and shell around a living kernel, threatening to stifle it, but there exists a kind of self-regulation by the living Christ's Holy Spirit: what is superfluous degenerates by itself; on the other hand, what is essential is transformed again into genuine life on being formulated. According to the profound words of Irenaeus, the Holy Spirit is perpetually rejuvenating the ecclesial vessel that contains the eternally youthful presence of Christ.

The same point could be made regarding *canon law*, a particular thorn in the side of many outsiders (as well as of people within the Church), who regard it as a stabilization of what actually ought always to be a purely charismatic event, as a relapse into Jewish absolutizing of the law, which Jesus and Paul have transcended and relativized. But what is the purpose of this element designed to organize and structure the ecclesial community, if not to keep it living and open to the presence of the one lawgiver, who has established a law of love, grace and mercy that is a supreme form of justice? "If you retain anyone's sins, they are retained": even an ecclesial law of punishment and penance is an aspect and function of this law of grace, whereby the law has to protect grace as well as to transmit it.

Office, sacraments, Scripture, tradition, canon law, all are concerned with the same thing: the form that the living content takes guarantees that the content will remain alive. In terms of the Church, this means that the institution is the condition for the possibility of Christ's genuine, personal presence.

Hence, on this higher, supernatural plane, the fundamental law of life, everything from plant to animal to man, is repeated: only in a complex organism can a life principle, a soul, grow and express itself. Therefore, the humorless bores who grumble about the ecclesial institution under the pretext of coming across the living kernel, direct encounter with Jesus, once the institution has been abolished, can be answered as Goethe answered the Philistines:

> Nature has neither kernel nor rind;
> It is everything at once, you'll find.
> But test yourself to try and see
> If rind or kernel you might be.

What Goethe says regarding nature, we say regarding the Church. His summons can just as well be applied to her: "Do not be so slow to see/ a sacred open mystery."

A few important conclusions now remain to be drawn from what we have said.

1. In certain respects, institution in the Church is similar to that in the purely human sphere; in other respects, it is dissimilar. Wherever free human persons live together, something comparable to institution, an accepted system of law, is necessary to protect their freedom. The free personality can develop only in order, not in anarchy. Anyone who would gainsay this aspect of the Church would see in her not an organic community willed by God but an empty, formal framework for purely private religious activity. This, of course, would directly contradict the gospel as well as the ecclesial image that inspired the first Christian communities and all subsequent ones.

However, though this human reason for institution in the Church is completely valid, it is by no means its proper justification. According to Paul's teaching, the faithful regard the ordered community as the "body" of Christ who is present. He becomes present above all in the sacraments he instituted, and then permits all who receive these sacraments in faith to share so really in his presence that, according to Paul, the individuals become members of his (mystical) body. This happens to each in keeping with his charism and his particular mission, just as the members of a body complement one another and are differentiated against the background of the whole. Here the view of the Church as original sacrament in the midst of the world, as *"sacramentum mundi"* receives its validity: the Church's external organization, which scandalizes so many, is none other than the manifestation of the vitality and viability of that great organic body, possessed and vivified by Christ present. This can also be recognized from the mysterious circulation between Eucharist and Church. The eucharistic Body of Christ, which becomes present in the liturgy of the community, draws the participating believers into the reality of Christ: "Is not the bread we break a sharing in the body of Christ? Because it is one bread, we, though many, are one body" (1 Cor 10:16f.). On the other hand, it is always the Church as the already existing body of Christ that renews the eucharistic presence of her Lord through the office bestowed on her: "The Eucharist makes the Church; the Church makes the Eucharist" (de Lubac).

2. We have said that institution exists in order to bring about the freedom of persons. The more

highly developed an organ is—for example, the human hand—the more the soul can do with it. The body as a whole limits the individual to being this particular place-bound and time-bound human being; simultaneously, however, it gives him freedom enabling him to make contact with all places and times, past, present and future. Being bound is at the same time the condition for a mobility that allows a spiritual soul to exert an influence far beyond itself. In a much higher sense, this is true of the Church as the presence of Christ. Because Christ is present in the mysterious organism of his Church, he is not on that account absent elsewhere in the world. To speak of the Church as *"sacramentum mundi"* means just the opposite: by virtue of his embodied presence in the Church, Christ permeates all of world history, as well as the existence of every human being. Nevertheless, this does not mean that he (as risen) is free to be and act anywhere he wishes, so that his ecclesial presence is entirely relative or superfluous. For the law of the Incarnation is not abrogated by the Resurrection: it operates in the witness to faith offered by specific human beings, in their life in common as a loving community, to which Scripture, sacraments and ecclesial law belong. All this brings the Church into relief as something unmistakably unique in the midst of humanity. But her prerogatives also entail a strict obligation:

as the body of Christ, the Church has the absolute duty of giving witness, through her example, to the world of this presence in her.

This witness ought to be the example of the love of Christians for one another and for all, and this in the unity of Christ, again expressly made visible and bonded together in the organized union of the parish with its pastor, the diocese with its bishop and the universal Church with the pope. An external, organized unity alone would not suffice as witness; it must be the expression of an inner unity of faith and love, if it is to become a convincing element of witness. On the other hand, living faith has no difficulty in adapting itself to the outward form of unity, whose sole purpose is to convert the subjectivity of a closed sect into the objectivity of a community that offers me not primarily the satisfaction of my religious longings but the presence of a Lord so exalted that I must above all submit, in adoration, to *his* will and saving plan for the world. Hence Christians owe the world the witness of mutual love in Christ as the only effective apologetics for the truth of Christianity. Everyone, even the most uneducated, can make a contribution here: "May they be one", prays the Lord, "as we (the Son and the Father) are one . . . that the world may believe that you have sent me and have loved them as you have loved me."

3. Furthermore, it must be expressly emphasized that, as the presence of Christ, ecclesial institution creates every desirable area of freedom for the individual Christian as well. This is not to say that he will be able to find Christ only where there is some explicit form of organization. Let us return to the example of the human body: the eye is an extremely subtle organ, but it looks out into the world without reflecting on itself; its glance is everywhere except on its own structure.

A citizen of one country needs a visa to go to certain other countries, but the eye can travel wherever it likes without need of a visa; the space extending to the stars is open to it. The same is true of the Christian. He can meet God and Christ everywhere: in the silence of direct prayer without any ecclesial liturgy; in encounters with his neighbor, who is an image of God and a real or potential temple of the Holy Spirit; in the midst of the din of a metropolis. Or when he opens Scripture, his meditating spirit, passing beyond the printed word, can become immersed in the depths of the divinity. The form is his point of departure and at the same time a sign indicating the right direction to take. "The truth will make you free." This is how it looks when seen from within, to anyone who experiences the institution as the presence of Christ; when seen from without, it seems like a cage. This leads us to the fourth and final point.

4. The institution of the Church, which from within is the presence of Christ and a liberating sphere, acts as a scandal to the world. And this very scandal is indispensable to prevent the Incarnation of God, and even his crucifixion, from dissolving into idealistic vapor and shallow morality. The Church, in her rigid structure, will always be a "stumbling block" for people. This expression from Isaiah in the Old Testament can, in a certain sense, also be applied to the Judaism always present in world history. Like the two sides of a coin, Israel and the Church belong together in a very mysterious, perhaps tragic way; together they witness to God's fidelity to his promises. In particular, the Church witnesses to Christ's fidelity to his own, his being with us always, to the very end.

Attempts have been made to exterminate Judaism, but that is impossible. Attempts will be made to decimate the Church, perhaps with success; but she will never be completely demolished. In our times an "assault on Christianity by the world religions" has been noted (G. Vicedom). Why? After they have drained off what seemed to be assimilable, the indigestible, annoying institution is left; it must disappear. But, as is well known, precisely the rind of a fruit contains the most vitamins. Life is in the living form itself. To cite Goethe again: "Neither time nor might dissolve / a set form, living as it evolves." The Church's form is not an end in itself but the *forma Christi*, present in the world and in world history, from which he will take effect in the whole. *He* is the form, not we. We only share in it, by grace, as servants of his cause. Human beings can add something peripheral to the institution of Christ— ballast, perhaps, which time erodes and washes away. But the living organism will never become ballast. Mere institution would be a mere lifeless corpse that would certainly have to be buried or cremated without delay. This, however, is not in the offing, for the body of which we are speaking is animated by an immortal soul, the Risen Lord, who does not let his body, the Church, die but wills to take it along with him into the resurrection of the body. Not that in eternal life the veil of the sacraments or the letter of Scripture or canon law will still be necessary, but they will not be annihilated either; they will be transformed into personal life, lived in the body. The world will not disappear in God; rather, the last sacrament will be the entire triune God revealed in the entirety of glorified creation.

FLIGHT INTO COMMUNITY

On every level of his being man is both an individual and a member of a community. Each of
these poles is related to the other: he is a personality
only if he is not closed in on himself but open to
his fellow men in service and self-giving; and he is
genuinely a community member only if he makes
his own independent contribution to the common
cause. This fruitful polarity is intensified in Christ's
Church, because on the one hand all together form
the one body of Christ and are integrated by
Christ the Head into a supernatural, organic unity
in him; and, on the other hand, in and beyond each
individual we are to recognize the Lord, who died
on the Cross for him personally as well as for me.
Hence the union of Christians by virtue of the
mystery of Christ is an especially mysterious and
intense one. This union binds all together, but in
such a way that it is also in each individual in an
unmistakable manner. But this ecclesial unity is
not the ultimate thing, for Christ died not only for
the members of the Church but for all men. This
means that behind every person I am to see his
Redeemer. In other words, every Christian has to
be open in a missionary sense to the non-Christian
world, even more intensely than the ecclesial com-

munity as such can be. The eucharistic assembly of Christians can be a sign or at best an invitation to the world, but in itself it is not mission; this is the duty of the individuals strengthened in the eucharistic assembly, sent forth from it and exposed to the world. Common prayer and the common celebration and reception of the Eucharist ought to have equipped all the members to go out and personally radiate what they have received, not as single individuals but as "ecclesial souls" (*animae ecclesiasticae*), either by an express proclamation or in the tacit preaching of their entire conduct.

The Christian's being exposed to the world belongs to the newness of Christianity in contrast to the Old Covenant. Even in those times, believers gathered in their common Temple only on solemn feasts, and for services in the synagogue only on the Sabbath. Between times, they normally lived in the national faith community of which they were a part and which attracted at most a few proselytes. The Church, on the contrary, may not form a closed faith community vis-à-vis the world. The Apostles were sent "into the whole world"; each Christian is likewise sent, in his own way. The liturgical assembly, as well as any other communal event in the Church and parish, always remains—at least among other things—oriented to training every individual to give witness before a non-Christian world. And after an age of relatively closed "Christendom", this is true again today more than ever.

Hence one can say that the practice of outwardly manifest ecclesial solidarity is meaningful in itself, and is so continually in the course of Christian existence. It is, however, essentially oriented to each participant's acquiring an inner ecclesiality; by means of the practice of external solidarity, each ought to become qualified to bear within himself a seed for creating new community.

Therefore, youth in particular is a time of intensive training in Christian attitudes by means of community experiences in prayer and liturgy, in order to help members of associations and leagues mature in self-reliant personalities. In the same way, basic communities will prepare the leaven that later effectively integrates into the community at large. And finally, the years of formation in an active or contemplative religious community ought to be a time of special training in the specific community spirit of the order, so that the individual member is enabled to take this spirit with him into the active apostolate or into contemplative solitude with God.

Precisely at this point, at which a person is required to move on, we not rarely find nowadays

hesitation and a standstill. This endangers an ecclesial community's specific thrust or at times
completely frustrates it. Various plausible excuses
for this hesitation are put forth: has the Church
not been through a period that was decidedly
individualistic in the liturgy as well as in personal
prayer and conduct? Did not a sense of church as
community first have to be reawakened—almost
by force—in people's hearts? Each one used to
perform his private devotions, even during the
eucharistic celebration, and regarded a mutual
opening of hearts almost as a profanation. Nevertheless (we shall add as an apology for this allegedly
very individualistic age), this period produced a
great number of outstanding personalities in public
life, both in the Church and in society. Can the
same be said of our community-happy generation?
Or are we mistaken in clearly detecting at the root
of this drive for community a fear of personal
uniqueness and solitude?

This fear, this anxiety, can be traced to the
whole character of our secularized and over-
technologized world, a world in which the individual no longer finds his way to God; he thinks
that in seeking God he will step out into emptiness
and cold, and so he looks for the needed nest-
warmth in the community. He likes to recall
Christ's words, "Where two or three are gathered

together in my name, I am there in their midst", as though Christ were present only in this case and not also when an individual seeks him in prayer.

It is deeply alarming to see a real flight from personal intimacy with God into the security of the community taking place in a great number of modern movements—youth movements first of all, but likewise groups of more mature persons who grow out of these youth groups. The intrusion of "group dynamics" even into the Ignatian Spiritual Exercises (intended by their founder to be essentially personal and made in silence) is symptomatic of many other things. No slightest objection can be made to charismatic groups or to communal exercises of prayer, nor to spiritualities that give central place to love of neighbor or the liberation of man by means of solidarity, provided that they pass without anxiety from external solidarity to nourishing the individual person with his inner, catholic dimension (that is, open to the global community). Were they not to do this, they would have to be accused of Christian infantilism. One sign that this accusation is not farfetched lies in today's tacit agreement that penitential services in common can completely, or almost completely, replace personal confession. At this point, precisely the most personal and most unrelinquishable act of the entire sacramental life is suppressed.

Since modern young people are so very afraid both to be alone with God and to be personally exposed to a faithless environment in his name, it remains fundamentally important that they undergo a religious community experience. But woe, if what are "ways and means" in this process were to be declared a permanent end in themselves.

On the level of youth groups the result would be that the young person, trained in group prayer, would never mature to spontaneous personal prayer and never hear that voice of God audible only in the "private room" mentioned in the Sermon on the Mount, the voice that would perhaps sound the decisive call to follow Christ personally and make known to the youth his life vocation.

On the level of the closed, integrated community, this would mean that the leaven, instead of fermenting in the Church, would have to turn sour in itself. This is somewhat evident in the dangerous and usually unsuccessful experiments in which Christian families, claiming to be "models" for the Church, form communes in their own blocks or settlements. But no one (and no community) in the Church is authorized to pass himself off as such a model, thinking he is turning the world into the Church, as it were, when he summons the world to adapt itself to this model. In a strange environment one might speak of "cells"; but in Christian terms, these would have to be effective in an apostolic (not propagandist) way in order to merit their name.

Social infantilism has the most devastating effect at the level of religious life, wherever the members think that they can and should replace christological obedience with a kind of democracy, naively imagining that by doing so the community would be obeying the voice of the Holy Spirit. The stark reality (soon felt) is that generally a majority, perhaps attained through manipulation, stifles the minority. Again, communal consultations and formations of opinion are to be held in honor; in the chapters of the ancient orders, they were taken for granted and always considered important for the abbot or superior in making his final decision. But to exclude the superiors and, with them, personal obedience, replacing them with collective acts, vitiates the vitality of the express promise that religious have made to follow Christ in his personal obedience to the Father's will, presented to him by the Holy Spirit as his "rule", even to the rigor of Gethsemane and Calvary. In the solitude of the christological as well as of the marian assent lies the fountainhead and source of every ecclesial community. Only they who do not shy away from returning to the source share fully in this community.

Community is always a gift made to those who courageously entrust themselves to God; and what community gives is, again, free access to the immediacy of its origin.

THE MYSTERY OF THE EUCHARIST

When we say that the Church is the body of Christ, the sociological analogy—multiplicity of members and of their functions in the unity of the living organism—is not the core of the statement. Either the words remain an image pointing to something else, or we must interpret them out of their deepest center. What is really meant and what remains a unique mystery over and beyond every analogy and every image is expressed in a passage such as the following: "The body is not for immorality but for the Lord, and the Lord for the body. . . . Do you not know that anyone united with a prostitute is one body with her, for 'the two', as it is said, 'become one flesh'. But anyone who is united to the Lord, is one *pneuma* with him" (1 Cor 6:13, 16f.). The first sentence forbids us to contrapose pneumatic oneness with the Lord to bodily oneness with a prostitute. Here, *pneuma* stands in contrast, not to body (*soma*), but to flesh (in the sense of originally sinful *sarx*, despite any allusion to the words spoken in paradise, for in our context fornication is being spoken of). In the same Pauline letter, the bodily (13) as well as pneumatic (17) unity of the entire human person with the entire person of the Lord is made clear by the expression "pneumatic body" (1 Cor 15:44). This is the body of "the second man coming from heaven", who—according to all the New Testament theologies—died and rose for us and to whom we are united by eating his Flesh and drinking his Blood. Church originates, still according to the same letter, in the incorporation of Christ's Body and Blood in each one who communicates with him at the eucharistic table. "The cup of blessing that we bless, is it not a sharing in the Blood of Christ? The bread that we break, is it not a sharing in the Body of Christ? Because there is only *one* bread, we though many are *one* body because we all share in this one bread" (1 Cor 10:16f.). Only after this central thought, which could not be expressed more clearly, does there follow what we called a sociological analogy in the beginning: that those who are one in the pneumatic body of Christ through Communion are related to one another as members of a unity that encompasses and vivifies them ("Christ is living in me": Gal 2:20). In the one *pneuma* all have been united into one body, and all were given one Spirit to drink (1 Cor 12:13).

But this is meant to be not the subject of, but only the prerequisite for our considerations. We will reflect first on the conditions under which the body of Christ became a eucharistic Body in which all the members of the Church can communicate, and second, on the consequences that ensue for one who communicates with the eucharistic Body.

1. Christ as Eucharist

The words of institution (we need not deal here with the different versions) provide the nearest point of departure for our first topic: "This is my Body which is given for you" (Lk 22:19); "This is my Blood . . . which is to be poured out for many" (Mk 14:24). "Given" clearly means the crucifixion, as its parallel, "poured out", shows; the Last Supper is an anticipation of the crucifixion.

And when the primitive Church and Paul can, from the fact of Jesus' Resurrection, draw the conclusion that the Cross meant salvation for all (this remained unrecognized during the event itself)—"He was given up for our sins and raised for our justification" (Rom 4:25)—this truth, as a "sacred open secret", is already manifest in the gesture with which Jesus offers his Flesh and Blood at table as "given" and "poured out". Chronologically, the gesture of self-giving precedes the violent Passion event and thus shows that his free self-surrender is also the essential reason and prerequisite for the fact that the subsequent horrible event can acquire its meaning of universal salvation. His free self-giving wants to go "to the end" (Jn 13:1); and the end is that self-disposition passes over into pure *letting* oneself be disposed of and *being* disposed of. The passivity of the Passion, with its fetters, scourging, crucifixion and piercing, is the expression of a supremely active will to surrender which for that very reason transcends the limits of self-determination into the limitlessness of letting oneself be determined. On the other hand, such a will to surrender, which gives itself—in the eucharistic gesture of self-distribution—beyond all the bounds of human finitude, would have to be regarded as promethean arrogance, were it not of itself the expression of a

114

prior state of being determined and being disposed of. Paul and John perceive this clearly in portraying the complete self-giving of Jesus to his own and to the world as the concretized self-giving of the Father, who, out of love for the world he created and in fidelity to his covenant with it, gives up what is most precious to him, his Son (Rom 8:32; Jn 3:16). Because Jesus is the one, the only one, who comes from above, from heaven, as Paul and John state, his Incarnation contains God's infinite will to give himself, which (as infinite) becomes manifest in his Son's fundamental will not to dispose anything by himself, but rather to put himself in all things at the disposal of the Father and his impelling Spirit. One can see that because of the Incarnation, the human reality of Jesus (his "flesh and blood" or his "life": Jn 10:15) is already predisposed to be eucharistic, insofar as it is God's personified gift to the world; and the realization of this self-giving at the Last Supper, the Passion and the Resurrection is nothing but the actualization of this self-giving that was always intended and really planned and initiated.

Before proceeding further, we should add that this self-giving in our fallen world was from the very outset meant to be soteriological: the Son is "sent" by the Father into the desolation of the Cross, because he really "takes upon himself" the sin of the world (Jn 1:29) and represents it in its entirety (2 Cor 5:14, 21; Gal 3:13; Eph 2:14–16). As mysterious as the "how" of this representation may remain, the fact of it may not be contested. Jesus' "for us" is by no means intended as a merely juridical, moral or satisfactory gesture but beyond that as something real, one could almost say "physical". It is my abandonment by God, which is inherent in my sin, and my dying apart from God and into the darkness of eternal death that he experiences in his "being delivered up"; and he experiences them more deeply and definitely than any mere creature can experience such things. No one but the only Son of the Father, whose food it is to do the Father's will, can definitively and matchlessly know and experience what it means to be deprived of this food and to undergo absolute, hellish "thirst" (Jn 19:28). His unique, hypostatic suffering embraces every temporal and eternal suffering possible to a created human being. On this account, he who was so definitively dead and lives forever holds "the keys of death and of hell" (Rev 1:18). Precisely through his being deprived of any food from God—and perhaps, as J. Jeremias thinks, Mk 14:25 (par.) actually also points to a voluntary eucharistic fasting by Jesus—God makes his Son food for the whole world. In suffering, his whole human substance is "made fluid" so that it can enter into human beings; but this takes place in such a way that at the same time he also makes fluid the boulders of sin that have formed in resistence to God's fluidity and dissolves them in that experienced godforsakenness of which they secretly consist.

Now the decisive point can be formulated. Jesus' eucharistic gesture of self-distribution to his Apostles, and through them to the world, is a definitive, eschatological and thus irreversible gesture. The Father's Word, made flesh, is definitively given and distributed by him and is never to be taken back. Neither the Resurrection from the dead nor the "Ascension" as "going to the Father" (Jn 16:18) are a countermovement to Incarnation, Passion and Eucharist. The farewell discourses bring this out clearly enough: I am going away, and shall return (Jn 14:28); you will see me, because I live and you will live (Jn 14:19). Or when Jesus says that he lays down his life in order to take it up again, that he lays it down of his own free will and has the power to lay it down and to take it up again (Jn 10:17–18), the addition of "I give them eternal life" (10:28) shows that there is no question of a taking back of what was given or of the gesture and the state of giving. The "liquefying" of Jesus' earthly substance into that of the Eucharist is irreversible; furthermore, it lasts not only (like a

117

"means") until "the end of the world", but is rather the blazing core around which (as in the vision of Teilhard de Chardin's younger days) the cosmos crystallizes, or better, from which it is set ablaze. One must realize what is theologically expressed in a profound way by portraying the risen Christ with the marks of his wounds: that the state of surrender during the Passion positively enters and is raised up into the now eternal state of Jesus Christ, and that between his "heavenly" state and his "eucharistic" state no difference can be posited that would affect their inner reality. When he leaves his destiny and the meaning and form of his redemptive work to the Father's good pleasure, to the Holy Spirit's interpretation and to the Church's further guidance and fruitfulness, Jesus' total self-surrender after giving himself at the Last Supper is so conclusive that it can never revert to self-disposition. And this is true even though, because of his obedience, he was "raised up as Kyrios" (Phil 2:11) and "made" such (Acts 2:30). He is "Lion" (Rev 5:5) only insofar as he is eternally standing before God's throne as the "Lamb as though slain" (Rev 5:6). This implies much more than that he merely stands before the Father as mediator in virtue of his acquired merits; likewise more than that he merely continues in an unbloody manner in heaven the "self-giving" he accomplished in a bloody manner on earth. It ultimately means that the Father's act of self-giving by which, throughout all created space and time, he pours out the Son is the definitive revealing of the trinitarian act itself in which the "Persons" are God's "relations", forms of absolute self-giving and loving fluidity. In the Eucharist the Creator has succeeded in making the finite creaturely structure so fluid—without fragmenting or violating it ("No one takes my life from me": Jn 10:18)— that it is able to become the bearer of the triune life. The "language" of human existence, in its spontaneity as well as in its subjection to the superior force of suffering and death, has as a whole become God's language and his self-expression. Of course, here we find ourselves at the center of the most impenetrable mystery, for we cannot conceive of a person as otherwise than holding himself within himself in order to give himself (this one who is with himself). And, in fact, the accounts of the Resurrection present just such a self-possessed one, who in supreme freedom and sovereignty lets himself be recognized when he pleases and likewise withdraws at will and issues commands with supreme authority. Yet this human being is at the same time the Word and the Son of the Father, who in surrendering his "form of God" has carried his kenotic self-giving to the utmost and does not nullify his self-giving, his surrender, his kenosis, but lets it be manifest as God's actual power and glory. The Crucified, and he alone, is the Risen One. For the privilege of thus giving himself he is forever thanking the Father as the Father's substantial Eucharist, which as such never becomes past and mere remembrance.

2. The Christian and the Eucharist

At this point there follows almost automatically what life in the Eucharist means to the believing receiver. Since the Eucharist expressly includes the utmost suffering (cf. the words of institution), but is also a function of the love of the Father (and of the entire triune God) which released the Son to suffer and raised him from the dead, every possible detail of the believer's life is caught up, supported and simultaneously enclosed in the Eucharist as an ecclesial, sacramental act. All of them belong within the same thanksgiving and hence also in the same celebration or feast. But this feast expressly embraces the whole of Christian existence—everything except sin—including by all means the apparently unfestive everyday life and even suffering, persecution and darkness deepening into the feeling of being forsaken by

God. Seen from the stance of the self-giving Lord, it is evident that sharing in his suffering is part of eucharistic fellowship with him. Not only Paul's writings but also the letters of the other Apostles are filled with this thought. It is not a question of self-appointed following of Christ, nor of ethico-ascetical imitation of his suffering, but of being disposed to follow the Lord, "being led where you would rather not go" (Jn 21:18). It is "grace" (1 Pet 2:19), not "work". While Lazarus is dead and the Lord is keeping his distance, Martha and Mary are led into a night of godforsakenness that they cannot understand ("Lord, if you had been here": Jn 11:21, 32) but which is imposed on them precisely as people who believe and love, in anticipation of the Cross to come.

Participation in the Eucharist takes place as a true "eating and drinking", which is a process of real transformation of another substance into one's own. Now, it is certainly correct to say that in this sacrament Christ transforms us into himself, rather than that we transform him into ourselves. And yet the process is more complex. In the Passion Christ transformed us into himself in taking our sins into himself. In the eucharistic event, however—if the symbol of eating and drinking is to be a fulfilled sign—it is the believer who offers the whole sphere of his life to the Lord who knocks, and places it at his disposal. This would mean that in the depths of our being the frontiers must now collapse for us too, as they collapsed— or, to put it better, proved to have been obsolete from the outset—for Jesus Christ in the course of his life and death. Above all, the boundary between oneself disposing (even in faith) and being at God's disposal must disappear. This is the essential eucharistic fluidity in which Jesus crosses the boundary into the actual Passion ("Not my will be done"), thus revealing the basic law of his existence that governed his entrance into this world ("I have come down from heaven, not to do my own will, but to do the will of the one who sent me": Jn 6:38). It is the boundary at which my free power of decision about limited things and actions for limited spaces of time surrenders to God's definitive disposition of me. This is both content and law of the "hour" (" 'What shall I say: Father, save me from this hour? But this is why I have come to this hour. Father, glorify your name!' Then a voice came from heaven, 'I have glorified it, and I will glorify it again' ": Jn 12:27f.). To allow this to happen in us by means of the Lord's presence in our own substance means to communicate in truth. It is the very "let it be done to me" of Mary that conforms us to the Son (according to his word).

This first elimination of a boundary necessarily leads to a second: removal of the line of demarcation between Passion and feast, Good Friday and Resurrection. For now the lawgiver in our human substance is he for whom real feasting consists in doing the Father's will, even unto abandonment by God. In dying on the Cross, he does not experience even the slightest trace of earthly festivity, any more than do Christians in concentration camps and other inhuman situations, not only of physical suffering but also of lack of spiritual communication. In the "form of God", the Son possesses every possible fulfilling communication with the Father in the Holy Spirit. But where the Son's love takes on the kenotic form of obedience out of love for the Father—thus beginning the form of the Eucharist—the Holy Spirit, who binds Father and Son, becomes the Spirit of the objective commission from the Father, the Spirit of the will to unconditional fulfillment of that mission in the Son. And this objectification of the Holy Spirit of love is the condition making possible the kenosis or, in other words, the opening of the inner divine love out into creation or, again, the transformation of the inner divine communication into eucharistic communion. The objectification of the Spirit of love is at the same time its transformation into an objective-ecclesial spirit, not to be measured by the criterion of personal religious experience, and for which, therefore, a wedding feast—between the Bridegroom Christ and the Bride Church—can be celebrated even where the individual believer detects little or nothing of it. What the individual experiences as desolation can, in the Holy Spirit of the Church, be consolation in the truest sense of the word. What the individual experiences as a break in communication and as desolate loneliness in the desert of an atheistic environment can, in the Holy Spirit of the Church, be the realization of communion, because communion cannot exist at all without including Christ's Cross, his abandonment by the Father, his breathing forth the Spirit and his descent into hell.

Here we find ourselves before the real depth of the Pauline paradox: "We are afflicted on all sides, but never [hopelessly] cornered; we are perplexed but never desperate; we are persecuted, but never forsaken; struck down, but never killed; we always carry with us in our body [*soma*] the dying of Jesus, so that the [resurrected] life of Jesus, too, may be manifest in our body" (2 Cor 4:8–10). This depth of assimilation of Christian existence to Christ's existence makes its appearance only where the trinitarian dimensions of the latter are not overlooked; for otherwise merely a private and moral relationship between the Christian and Christ (which never exists in isolation) would be visible and not its ecclesial and sacramental fullness and prerequisite. What Paul describes in this passage is eucharistic experience: how the surrendered body of Christ becomes the inner law of Paul's body (i.e., of his concrete existence) and how the Eucharist transforms Paul's bodily existence into an ecclesial existence—in short, into a member of Christ's body. But inasmuch as the Eucharist is inseparable from the Church, and the Church is given to "drink" of the Holy Spirit of the Father and the Son, the personal relationship of the believer to Christ has already expanded into the trinitarian sphere. The Eucharist itself is never the private relationship of the receiver to Christ; rather, it is receiving the Father's gift, the Son, in the Church.

This is the ultimate reason why suffering experienced on the personal level can be regarded as belonging to festive celebration on the ecclesial-sacramental level. The "wedding feast" (Mk 2:19; Mt 22:1ff.; Jn 2:1ff., 3:39) is the all-encompassing totality, prepared by God the Father together with the Son and the Spirit, carried out in death and Resurrection, in Church and Eucharist; while "fasting" (Mk 2:20), being judged (Mt 22:11ff.), the embarrassment of the empty jars (Jn 2:3) and of other insufficient food (Jn 6:7 par.), the "decreasing" (Jn 3:30) are always partial moments within the festive picture. It is the Baptist who speaks of his decrease, his radical renunciation in view of the increasing and fulfilling Lord, in connection with his "complete joy" that the Bridegroom Christ has found the Bride Church (Jn 3:29). The precursor's "decrease", his bodily and mental suffering, makes room for the wedding feast that is taking place, and this act of making room itself has a profoundly eucharistic character. Kenosis is an emptying out to provide a space that can be filled, and the Eucharist is the permeation of the kenosis with God's love being poured out in it as flesh given up and blood shed. In the Eucharist, however, there no longer exists the difference that still existed between the Baptist (Old Covenant) and Jesus (New Covenant) in which the one "decreases" so that the other can "increase". Now there is identity between the kenosis—the renunciation that the Son's love made of its divine form—and the triune God's love poured out over all space and time: this identity is, in itself and in us, the Eucharist.

THE WORTHINESS OF THE LITURGY

It is only with fear and trembling that we can approach this theme. What human liturgy could be "worthy" of the object of its veneration, before whom even in heaven all beings fall prostrate, remove their wreaths and crowns and lay them in a gesture of adoration before God's throne: "You alone are worthy, Lord our God, to receive glory and honor and power" (Rev 4:11)? This return in heaven of all honor received from creatures to him "who created everything by his will" can only bring a community of sinners on earth spontaneously to its knees, acknowledging, "Lord, I am not worthy." It would be an odd deception, however naive, if the members of this community, assembled to praise and honor God, were to have any other purpose than the act of perfect adoration and self-surrender: for instance, their own edification or some undertaking or other in which they themselves, alongside the Lord who should be receiving their homage, become thematic.

In a purely monotheistic religion, the gesture of prostration is the most perfect expression of the entire person's surrender, even in large gatherings. What Christian can view the crowd in silent adoration in a mosque without being deeply moved?

In the religion of the Covenant, listening to God's word, the Torah, has central place: God speaks and man obediently receives, searching with all his heart for the correct response. This may be accompanied by symbolic rites, such as the Passover meal, eaten standing and at the point of departure, the last strengthening nourishment before setting out into the desert to follow God's guidance.

But then, in the trinitarian religion, there is the enormous transformation: the sheep eaten in the family circle gives way to "the Lamb slain before the foundation of the world", "that takes away the sins of the world" and gives his Flesh and Blood as "real food and real drink". One can understand those heretics (even if one likewise understands their being condemned) who recoil from the excess of this divine mystery, imploring the faithful not to demean what is ineffable and fear-inspiring, mindful of the words of Paul: "Anyone who eats the bread or drinks the Lord's cup unworthily will be guilty of the Lord's body and blood. Therefore, let a man examine himself", lest he "eat and drink judgment" (1 Cor 11:27–29). God himself encourages us, even presses us, to "eat the Flesh of the Son of Man and drink his Blood" (Jn 6:53), if we want to attain to eternal life. We can do this,

128

however, only if we are mindful of the "awesome exchange"[1] between our guilt, which he bears, and his innocence, which he gives us on the Cross. In receiving him into ourselves, we recall that he has taken us into himself in his Passion and that, as Augustine repeatedly says, we receive the physician who heals us by our having caused his death: "For whenever you eat this bread and drink the cup, you proclaim the Lord's death, until he comes" (1 Cor 11:26). Nevertheless, we are not to approach the Lord's table embarrassed and down-cast, for the Lord who wants to come to us calls us his friends (for whom he has died: Jn 15:13). He does not want us to "act like strangers" (as the disciples do at the meal by Lake Tiberias: Jn 21:12), but to open ourselves to receive the Father's gift. For in celebrating the liturgy, our gaze is not restricted to Jesus, but is raised to him from whom ultimately the highest of all good gifts comes: to the Father. Nor do we open our hearts and raise our minds heavenward of ourselves, but in the power of the Holy Spirit of the Father and of the

---

[1] *Phrikton synallagma* is the term used by Proclos of Con-stantinople (d. 446) in his first sermon on Mary (PG 65, 688 D; cf. Martin Herz, "Sacrum Commercium", in: *Münchener Theologische Studien II*, vol. 15 [Zink, 1958], 71), which corresponds to the Latin *admirabile* (or *sacrum*) *commercium*.

Son poured into our hearts. It is solely in view of the entire triune God that the worshipping community is gathered together to celebrate God's generosity and liberality.

God's glory, the majesty of his splendor, comes with its most precious gifts to us who are to "praise the glory of his grace" (Eph 1:6). This last summons constitutes the norm and criterion for planning our liturgical services. It would be ridiculous and blasphemous to want to respond to the glory of God's grace with a counter-glory produced from our own creaturely reserves, in contrast to the heavenly liturgy that is portrayed for us in the Book of Revelation as completely dominated and shaped by God's glory. Whatever form the response of our liturgy takes, it can only be the expression of the most pure and selfless reception possible of the divine majesty of his grace; although reception, far from signifying something passive, is much rather the most active thing of which a creature is capable.

Our first question is: what is excluded from such active reception? Our second is: what form can this reception take? As we shall see, the answers to these questions are not always tidily separable, because forms that may be expressions of pure reception in certain people could become mani-

festations of self-admiration and worldly grati-
fication in others.

Certainly, everything that distracts the congregation from paying attention to God and his
coming and makes it revert to itself must be
excluded—except at the moment of examination
of conscience, at the confession of guilt and at the
Domine, non sum dignus. Anything solemn and
ceremonial that does not direct hearts and minds
to the one being solemnized is evil, in proportion
to how much the character of the solemnity becomes detached from its object and becomes itself
the center. Now we have arrived at the ambiguity,
of which we shall cite more detailed examples:
that in praising God a person directs back to
himself what is reserved for God alone—the praise
of his glory— so that a part of its luster redounds
to himself. It often happens (and the danger seems
to be even greater nowadays than in former times)
that a liturgical assembly measures the success of a
celebration by the degree of its own edification,
the extent to which the participants "take part"
and are "moved" by it, instead of letting itself be
moved by God and his gifts and letting him "take
over". There are congregations that, perhaps un-
consciously, celebrate themselves rather than God;
and this is equally true of traditional and of progressive groups, of liturgies in long-established

parishes as well as the freely formed services so popular among young people. This means that the criterion of the "vitality" of a liturgical service also remains highly ambiguous; it is always a question of whether it effects a vital opening and conversion of hearts or the private enjoyment of one's own vitality. Naturally, this ambiguity comes to light in an especially acute way in the homily or sermon, which ought to have only one aim: to direct everyone's attention (including that of the homilist) to the mystery being celebrated in its inexhaustibly manifold aspects, and not to allow any of the divine luster to redound in the process to the speaker and what he is saying.

The problem becomes compounded when the correct thought is expressed that the joy of man who is redeemed and blessed beyond measure mingles with the seriousness of the "sacred exchange" which we celebrate. How both Cross and Resurrection can be experienced together in Christian life is a profound enigma, and the explanations of it are by no means unequivocal. There exists a simultaneity: deep, hidden, perhaps hardly perceptible joy in the midst of a sorrow that can completely engross a person; there is also an alteration of phases in Christian life, like the way in which changes of weather or seasons succeed one another. In a parish communal liturgy, a reverential awareness of the gravity of the mystery together with joy over it must be expressed in a manner appropriate to the objectivity of the mystery being celebrated, though it is true that human joy can find different modes of expression in different peoples or even in people of different ages. Once again the ambiguity comes into play: expressions of joy that are genuine praise of God, are intended as such and can be understood as such by others belong to the sphere of appropriate expressions of liturgical prayer; on the contrary, whatever verges on subjective ecstasy does not. (It is easy to distinguish the subtle symbolism, restrained to the last detail, of oriental cultic dances from those that serve to enrapture both dancer and spectators.) Authentic Christian joy can be expressed in the way a congregation sings in unison, the way a priest says the prayers of the canon or the orations, the way a deacon delivers the sacred texts; and the Christian heart of the people can immediately distinguish this authenticity from everything that is outwardly contrived and rhetorical and perhaps inwardly bored. Let no one think that giving primacy to objectivity dispenses the subject from making his contribution. This will have been best made when everyone senses that the subject is totally at the service of the mystery.

An element lacking in good taste has crept into the liturgy since the (falsely interpreted) Council, namely, the joviality and familiarity of the celebrant with the congregation. People come, however, for prayer and not for a cozy encounter. Oddly enough, because of this misinterpretation, one gets the impression that the post-conciliar liturgy has become more clerical than it was in the days when the priest functioned as mere servant of the mystery being celebrated. Before and after the liturgy, personal contact is entirely in place, but during the celebration everyone's attention should be directed to the one Lord.

The tendency of a congregation to celebrate itself instead of God will increase, imperceptibly but unfailingly, if its faith in the reality of the eucharistic event wanes. When an almost rudimentary Church, gathered to await her Lord and to let herself be filled by him, considers herself from the outset as a church to which nothing essential can be added, the eucharistic celebration will degenerate into mere symbolism and the congregation will be celebrating nothing but its own piety which existed already and feels corroborated by the community's repeated gathering. When this happens, pharisaism is imminent. Conversely, when those assembled feel in their inmost hearts their urgent need of the Lord's coming among and in them if they are to grow together into a true Church in which each member is imbued with the Church's sentiments, then what happens objectively will arouse a corresponding subjective response. The worthiness of the liturgy increases in proportion to the participants' awareness of their own unworthiness. It is impossible, then, to manipulate or technically produce this worthiness: if the Christian attitude of (the majority of) the congregation and of the priest is genuine, the celebration is "worthy".

Here, however, we can observe a curious phenomenon—and this brings us, without perceptible transition, to the second point. There are objectively worthy "forms" of liturgical prayer, which of course could have evolved only in eras of authentic subjective attitudes of prayer: for example, our venerable canons, collects and other Mass prayers, which through centuries of subjective prayer have acquired a new dimension of dignity. And now there are some who think that to let themselves be sustained by these forms, to entrust themselves to centuries of other men's prayers, would guarantee them in advance the correct subjective attitude. But they deceive themselves in this regard. For them the dignity of the form—a perhaps wonderfully polished, aesthetic dignity—predominates

135

over the perennially new, nonobjectifiable dignity of the divine event. The awareness of inherent glory gave inspiration to works of incomparable earthly beauty in the great tradition of the Church. But these works become suitable for today's liturgy only if, in and beyond their beauty, those who take part are not merely moved to aesthetic sentiments but are able to encounter that glory of God to which the Creator wanted to lead such works.

Among these works we can name not only Gregorian chant, the work of Palestrina and his contemporaries, and a good part of the old German (chiefly Protestant) church hymns, but also Bach's High Mass, Haydn's Masses, Mozart's Litanies and—a high point of musically expressed faith— the uncompleted Credo of his Mass in C Minor and the Kyrie of Schubert's Mass in E Major. If the singers of such works really pray them, the music can transmit something of the true original inspiration to listeners whose sensory apparatus is attuned not only to the beautiful but to the holy and the divinely glorious.[2] Those who hear only

[2] My multiple-volume work, *Herrlichkeit*, attempted to work out the distinction in niveau between intramundane beauty and the divine glory. In speaking of God, the Hebrew word *kâbôd*, which has been rendered with *doxa* in Greek and with *gloria* in Latin, likewise means might, importance, and

the beautiful and are moved only by that can have a quasi-religious experience—like the many who listen to Saint Matthew's Passion on Good Friday— but they are deceived regarding the true meaning of what they are hearing.

Whether "beautiful" liturgy (which, in order to be beautiful, certainly does not need Latin, which cannot be understood by most people) is beautiful only for certain generations, while succeeding generations are no longer able to appreciate its beauty, can remain an open question. "What is beautiful must also die", and embalming does not help it. But on no account may it be replaced by anything ugly or vulgar, trivial or empty; the best alternative would be something plain that need

---

dignity in the sense of majestic splendor. *Doxa* and *gloria* do not fully transmit the original meaning (H. Schlier translates it with *Machtglanz*). In treating here of the dignity of the liturgy, we mean in the first place that it should communicate a presentiment of the divine *kâbôd*; this can be translated into a worldly beauty, which can be either very plain and simple or ornate. It is said that beauty is disinterested; hence, it would seem that it cannot be "used" for religious purposes in the liturgy. But this is a sophism. For the divine glory is the most disinterested thing possible, as it circulates within the divine triunity and then flows out into the world. There is therefore no excuse for remaining on the level of aesthetics (or for mourning over old forms of the Mass), for in the liturgy everything is relative to and oriented toward God's glory.

not be inferior in dignity to those earthly grandeurs that are no longer intelligible. "Blessed are the poor in *pneuma*", if only they admit their poverty and do not try to camouflage it. If a generation is not able to provide any authentic religious images for the Church, it should not claim that bare walls more effectively concentrate the spirit on what is essential. If we have become small people, we should not try to reduce the mystery we are celebrating to our own size. And if we have to a great extent lost our sense of dignity, our profession of faith should nevertheless have helped us to retain enough sense of God's majesty that, on encountering it, we will still feel our distance from it—greater eras may have felt it more strongly—and behave properly toward God.

Lay people will frequently be able to do this more directly than the pastor and his assistant, who become confused by the many cheap pastoral aids; in such cases it is the laity's duty to protest against unworthy accretions and to insist on their legitimate desires for authenticity in the liturgy. But let no one too hastily claim to play the role of *arbiter elegantiarum* in the Church. The real arbiter of the dignity of the liturgy is the "simple heart", the "single eye".

The Christian knows something more: that the assembly of God's people is never a mere mass-meeting, but the gathering together of individuals who by their call to follow Christ and their baptism in Jesus' death are "called together" to solitude with God—"strangers in this world"—and to commonality in the sharing of the one bread and the one cup. Both aspects of Christian existence are indispensable and must always be able to find articulation. Liturgy is the act, not of an anonymous "Church", but of a group of persons, whose relationship to Christ makes them persons qualitatively. This must be taken into consideration in planning the liturgy. The pre-conciliar liturgy was often the random coming together of individuals in one place, with each one absorbed in his own devotions; since the Council, it is still oftener the assembling of those who let themselves be carried along on the waves of a purely social event and largely forego personal prayer, or perhaps are forced to forego it on account of the uninterrupted talking of the celebrant and singing of the crowd. And they do so regretfully, because amid the stress of daily life and the noise of city blocks people can find neither a place nor time for personal prayer. Nowadays the liturgy must take this into account, not only for pedagogical reasons but also and above all for theological ones. Communal prayer and singing ought to leave room for individual recollection: before the collect (whose name indicates that it is a summary of the personal petitions of the individuals), after the homily, after Communion. And the celebrant should give meaningful suggestions as to how one can use the time of silence, so that it will not turn out to be a mere waiting for things to move again.

By his earnestness and readiness to pray, each person shares the responsibility for bringing about a worthy liturgy. Texts from the first centuries of Christianity clearly witness to this. The unique quality of a Christian assembly for celebrating the Eucharist is a guarantee that it is possible to thank the eternal Father for showing the world and each individual in it, by means of the gift of his Son, how much he "is love".

CHRISTIAN AND
NON-CHRISTIAN MEDITATION

The author of this work is writing as a Christian theologian, and only as such. Like every Christian who tries to live his faith, he has certain Christian experiences; but he has none in non-

Christian meditation. In some respects this is an awkward point of departure, especially since it is evident that Eastern meditation (with which we are principally concerned here) has very much more technical know-how and method at its command than does Christian meditation, just as an acrobat knows how to do many more stunts than an ordinary person does. Nevertheless, a Christian theologian should be entitled a priori to make certain statements about the relationship between Christian and non-Christian meditation, first of all because of the classification of meditation in itself (and the techniques belonging to it) on both sides. In his basic work *Asiatische Gottheit —Christlicher Gott*[1] [Asian godhead-Christian God], Jacques Albert Cuttat posed the decisive question of the supreme values in both spheres. In so doing, he came to the conclusion that the practitioner of Eastern meditation who has attained the highest degree of enlightenment, and is therefore characterized as the supreme religious type, should not be seen as a counterpart to the Christian "mystic" (such as Eckhart or John of the Cross) as

[1] Einsiedeln: Johannes Verlag, 1971. The French original, "L' Expérience chrétienne est-elle capable d'assumer la spiritualité orientale?", in *La Mystique et les mystiques*, ed. A. Ravier (Paris: Desclée de Brouwer, 1965).

a comparable supreme type, but to the saint, who may or may not be a mystic. If this is correct, then the Christian theologian has a right to ask:

First, when a master in meditation is elevated to the rank of a human religious supreme value—this is obviously connected with a certain world view and metaphysics—how is this to be judged from a Christian viewpoint?

Second, what religious status does the respective method of meditation receive where (that is, in Christianity) the non-Christian scale of values as such is disputed? The answer to the second question will depend on whether and to what extent the non-Christian techniques of meditation are dependent on, or can be made independent of, the final goals that they possess in a world view such as Buddhism, for example.

The Question of Supreme Values

Regarding the first question, that of supreme values, three answers are possible; of these, only the third comes under consideration for us. The first, that of the Eastern world views, recognizes the Christian way as merely one among many (cf. the experiments of Ramakrishna); it does not accept Christianity's claim to be absolute. The second, that of the history of religion, allows every form of religion its own highest values and endeavors to produce a (humanistic) synthesis that is superior to or at least a synopsis of all the systems. This idea of a synopsis is theologically impracticable for the Christian. He must do two things: determine the conditional value of the Eastern global world view within the absolute value of Christian revelation, and, relatively independent of this, classify the Eastern methods of meditation.

The most diverse options are available at this point. Some believe that yoga methods, being neutral as far as any world view, can be made usable for both religious systems;[2] insofar as the methods originated in the East, these authors work to "de-orientalize" them.[3] Others seem to go a step further, into the philosophy of religion, and in addition to the methods also endorse to a great extent an interchangeability of content.[4] Still

[2] J. M. B. Déchanet, *Christian Yoga* (New York: Harper and Row, n.d.).

[3] Klemens Tilmann, *Die Führung zur Meditation* (Einsiedeln: Benziger, 1974).

[4] Above all K. Graf Dürckheim (e.g., in: *Zen und wir* [Fischer, 1974]) and to a large extent H. Enomiya-Lassalle, *Zenmeditation, eine Einführung* (Einsiedeln: Benziger, 1975). Vis-à-vis Carl Albrecht, Enomiya-Lasalle would insist on an assimilation of the person by the apersonal in the experiential

others maintain in varying degrees the irreducibility of content and, therefore, also of method, although they perceive strong analogies between Christian and non-Christian methods and ways or recommend the use of some Eastern methods in an adapted form.[5] For still others, the divergences are greater;[6] even someone who feels called to meditate entirely within the Indian setting[7] meditates from the viewpoint of Christianity's deepest mysteries, the Trinity and the Sonship of God, and meticulously distinguishes the applicability of Eastern methods.[8] Finally, there is the unique and impressive research of the Christian physician, Carl

---

sphere (102), although as a Christian he ought to hold the opposite ontically. Though Heinrich Dumoulin, in *Östliche und christliche Mystik* (Freiburg: Alber, 1966), largely agrees with the way of Zen, he is aware of "the basic insufficiency" characteristic of all the branches of Buddhist religion: because of the "lack of clarity" in knowledge of God: "full justice is not done to the human personality either" (222).

[5] For example, Yves Raguin, *Chemins de la contemplation: Eléments de la vie spirituelle* (Paris: Desclée de Brouwer, 1969); English trans. *Paths to Contemplation* (Abbey Press, 1974).

[6] Jürg Wunderli, *Schritte nach innen: Östliche Meditation und westliche Mystik* (Freiburg: Herder, 1975).

[7] Such as the great pioneer of meditation, Jules Monchanin, who can be compared to Charles de Foucauld. See Henri de Lubac, *Images de l'abbé Monchanin* (Paris: Aubier, 1966).

[8] Jules Monchanin, *Mystique de l'Inde, mystère chrétien* (Paris: Fayard, 1974), especially the chapter "Yoga chrétien?", 241ff.

Albrecht, who formulates an exact psychology and phenomenology of the state of concentration and in so doing knows how to distinguish genuine mystical experience (the fundamentally Christian one) from other phenomena.[9]

In fact, if with Jacques Albert Cuttat we hold that man's relationship to God within Christian revelation is qualitatively different from other relationships and at the same time embraces them, it will be logically correct to consider the methods used, not in neutral fashion, but in light of the particularity of the phenomenon; nevertheless, one can speak of a (critical) "assumption" of all of Eastern spirituality together with its methods, and thereby insist on retaining the contrast as well as the convergence right to the end. Because of the limited space available to us, we must, unlike Cuttat, confine ourselves to a few concise points.

[9] Schünemann, *Psychologie und mystisches Bewusstsein* (Bremen, 1951); *Das mystische Erkennen* (Bremen, 1958). Posthumously there appeared *Das mystische Wort: Erleben und Sprechen in Versunkenheit*, ed. H. A. Fischer-Barnicol (Mainz: Grünewald, 1974), with a significant and cautious introduction by Karl Rahner. He rightly calls attention to the lack of agreement in Catholic theology regarding the essence and limits of the concept of mysticism. See also my treatise "Zur Ortsbestimmung christlicher Mystik", in Werner Beierwaltes et al., *Grundfragen der Mystik*, Kriterien 33 (Einsiedeln: Johannes Verlag, 1974), 37–71.

According to what we have already said, we can develop our material in three steps. First of all, each party will explain itself: its point of departure, its paths and goals. Let it be noted in advance that in this first section only *religious* goals of meditation will be under consideration. This means that the following are excluded: purely physical training (such as breathing exercises, bodily position), as well as psychological exercises aimed at promoting general well-being, balance or relaxation from the stress occasioned by the demands of daily life: in this category we can include the comprehensive cultural fact that people in the West who begin to experience technologized civilization as unbearable and meaningless need an infusion from the East to restore the anthropological balance. Though all this may be true and valuable, it remains below the threshold of the religious objective: the search for the Absolute, for God. It can even serve private or collective egoisms; only when it transcends these does it become important for us. Secondly we shall ask whether and how and according to which scale of values Eastern methods of meditation can be integrated into Christianity. Thirdly, a Christian remainder will result, consisting of whatever cannot be overtaken and dealt with by any method of meditation.

146

Before we begin to speak of Eastern and Western methods of meditation, a preliminary remark is in order. It is a striking fact that nowhere in the Scriptures of the Old and New Covenants is there even the slightest mention of a technical instruction for meditating. All one can say is that room for meditation, in a broad and indefinite sense, is provided—for example, when the "first Commandment" is enjoined: "Hear, Israel, the Lord our God is *one* Lord; and you shall love the Lord your God with your whole heart, with your whole soul and with all your strength. . . . And these words shall be written in your heart, and you shall enjoin them on your children and shall speak of them when you are sitting at home and when you are walking on the road, when you lie down and when you arise. You shall bind them on your hand as a reminder and bear them on your forehead as a sign."[10]

Both the intensity and the exteriority of this prescription are deepened to a certain degree in what the Psalms[11] refer to as "meditating" and in what a softly murmured, repetitive reciting of

[10] Dt 6:4ff.
[11] Ps 1:2; Ps 63:6; Ps 77:12; Ps 143:5.

147

a Scripture passage implies: something that continues to be operative in the "Jesus Prayer" of Byzantine hesychasm and on into the writings of the Russian pilgrim. (The Byzantines also practice a prayer synchronized to the rhythm of the breath; and in the *Spiritual Exercises* of Ignatius of Loyola, no. 258ff., this form of prayer finds a place.)

It is not recorded anywhere that Jesus practiced meditation exercises with his disciples; he teaches them a simple vocal prayer. We do not yet know how he prayed during his solitary hours of prayer. In several places, Paul speaks of "unceasing prayer" (and Luke must have taken this expression from him and inserted it into his Gospel: 18:1); since then, this directive has met with the most varied interpretations. Of itself, biblical revelation demands that one take time for the God who has shown himself to be so wondrous and incomprehensible in Jesus Christ; to wonder and to give thanks that God's sovereignty abased itself to such an extent; to make the response that surges up to this ever greater God of "foolish" love. Throughout the centuries, there is no end to suggestions on how one ought to expose oneself to this love of God and respond to it. But none of these suggestions has ever solidified into a method that is obligatory for the individual.

A. Eastern Meditation

In the East, what was formerly the common property of all peoples—the religious element as distinguishing mark of the human—stands out most clearly and most representatively for modern mankind. It has a starting point, a path and a goal. If this religious element remains dependent on its own resources, it tends in its search for the Absolute to confer an absolute character even upon the circumstances of this search.

a. The *starting point* is the fundamental religious experience that the world of appearances that surrounds us, of which our empirical "I", our character and everyday conduct are also a part, cannot possibly be the ultimate, absolute reality. The primordial religious experience is that of a cleft between the ground of being and ourselves, a scattering of what is basically one, an alienation (according to Plato and Plotinus we are living in a *regio dissimilitudinis*, a region of dissimilarity). Alienation also implies unfreedom and entanglement. If this fluctuating experience is made an absolute, the "world of appearances" becomes mere "illusion" (*maya*), an entanglement becomes one's fate, and perpetual mere becoming is a hopeless cycle (*samsara*).

b. Therefore religious longing, the "restless

heart", sets out on a journey, if possible in the footsteps of a wise man who has found a way to freedom and can teach it to others. There is a *met'hodos*, a following (*met*) of a way (*hodos*), which is a "path of instruction" (*dhamma-pada*). The way—absolutized in its own right—is radical: it leads from the exterior into the interior, from the din of multiplicity into the silence of oneness; it excavates what is clogged up, so that the original spring may flow once again. A person who takes the initiative in this regard must "exercise" himself (*askesis* simply means "exercise"), above all in renunciation.

c. The goal can be none other than to touch, to encounter, to enter into the sphere of the Absolute, of the origin of all, of the nonstrange, of "home"; it is the elimination of duality. It is absolutized in Shankara's vedantism of *advaitya*, "nonduality", or in other (of course, always somehow groping) formulas of the coincidence of that which is inmost in man (whether it be called *atman*, *purusha* or something else) and that which is ultimately all-embracing (Brahman).

In the initial stages, the Absolute can possess personal characteristics; in the early stage, the still individual human person can pray to an individual divine person, entrust himself to him, and so forth. But since "religion", seen as a human quest, regards a person as possessing the characteristics of human limitation, these personal traits and modes of acting disappear in the final stages of a depersonalized experience. Hence, in this context, one can speak only of "guilt" (that somehow is at the root of alienation and together with it is overcome by degrees), never of "sin" against a God who is ultimately personal.

B. Biblical Christian Faith

Biblical revelation is not a variety of the religion described above, which would serve as its anthropological basis, but a response *from above* to it. Everything proceeds from God's free initiative, and everything (including the world and the ego) is explained in its light. Consequently, guilt appears as what it really is, namely, sin; and God's self-revelation appears as a free grace.

a. The God of Abraham, Moses and Christ is the free Creator of the world, which he affirms as "very good"—regardless of how it may look to us. Thus, its being other than God does not automatically amount to alienation and unreality. Beyond the actual state of the creature, including my own ego, there is a will that affirms and confirms the creature, you and me, in this actual state. God sees this creature, this I and Thou, as valuable and lovable the way it is. This implies two things for the creature: first, that it owes its creaturely existence to this external will (whose creative motive can ultimately be only love).

In order to clarify this, let us insert one of Fénelon's meditations, to which there have been numerous parallels in Christian tradition since Augustine:

> There was nothing in me that preceded all his gifts and that could have served as a vessel to receive them. The first of his gifts, the basis of all the others, is that which I call my own "I": God has given me this "I"; I owe him not merely everything I have but also everything I am. O unprecedented gift, so readily proclaimed in our weak language, but never understood in all its profundity by the human spirit! . . . Without God I would not be I; I would have neither the "I" that I could love nor the love with which I love this "I", nor the will that loves it, nor the thought by which I know myself. Everything is gift, and he who receives the gifts is himself first of all a gift received.

But then it is true that the "I", knowing that it is affirmed and loved by the eternal "I", must in the end affirm itself to be one to whom God says

"Thou" in an absolutely personal relationship that cannot be confused with the relationship I may cultivate with any other human person. The always unique God calls me by my unique, unrepeatable name. But this means that the biblical God is Creator in order to reveal himself; and, as a consequence, creation is the foundation of his self-communication. And man's quest for God (transcendence) is the prerequisite, built into creation, for God's being "accepted" by man, for his being understood and received. If this is so, then man's authentic search for God is not a denial or rejection of his finitude, but a process of making himself free and ready to be completely seized and possessed by God.

Though this process is something active (in this respect comparable to the religious "method"), it must nevertheless increasingly take into account the essential freedom of the God who comes to meet man. Therefore it is essential to the bibilical-Christian method that the person be thoroughly aware that no practice and no form of readiness on his part can effect or compel God's coming. Thus the Christian way to God must necessarily include the experience of *"desolatio"*, the nonexperience of God's coming. At one time I can be granted an experience of God's self-bestowal and nearness, at another time not; in both cases my degree of inner purity and readiness can be the same. According to Jesus' parables, one simply has to be vigilant without knowing when the Lord or Bridegroom will come.

b. Since God as free Creator and Revealer is personal, guilt, which now appears as "sin" (over against his absolute love), plays an entirely different role. Alienation is not merely a case of nonidentity with the Absolute but of estrangement from absolute Love because of egoism, deification of a creature, disobedience to a divine command, or something similar. This estrangement is a loss of divine love, which is not available to me as an actual possibility, in order to return to God. It is true that the prodigal son sets out to return to his father, but only because, like an unknown treasure, the knowledge of his father's fatherliness is not lost but is still present in him. Conversion is not a "technique"; rather, it is an act that as a whole is due to the all-embracing initiative of divine love and is also conscious of its indebtedness.

c. Grace is God's self-bestowal, not in order merely to put himself on exhibition, but in order to share himself. This Christian sharing in the divine Being extends all the way to the mystery of a new birth from the paternal bosom of the

Godhead[12] to being a child of the Father-God. This far exceeds mere createdness, yet without invalidating it. Otherwise I would no longer be I. On the indestructible foundation of "greater dis-similarity"[13] there rises a dizzying similarity.[14] God cannot possibly be objectified; he is always the Thou of our I and We, a limitless Super-Thou, who, being the ever-greater one over us, eternally claims our *adoration*. Adoration is not identification; this is made clear to us by the glimpses into the realm of eternal blessedness given us in the Book of Revelation at the end of the Bible. But in the midst of adoration, the "wedding feast of the Lamb" is also mentioned—the nuptials between heaven and earth, God and creature—signifying God's complete advent in the world.[15] In the concluding symbols, all the water of salvation flows from his throne, making all the fruits of immortality grow. God is the only light, the only temple; his countenance is completely unveiled; his name is written on the foreheads of the saved. These are images intended to convey that the

[12] Jn 1:13; 3:3, 5.

[13] "Maior dissimilitudo": Fourth Lateran Council.

[14] "Now we are God's children, and what we shall one day be has not yet been revealed. We know that when it is revealed, we shall be like him. . ." 1 Jn 3:2.

[15] "That God may be all in all": 1 Cor 15:28.

lasting adoration in the distance confirms all the more profoundly and completely the mystery of union.

According to the foregoing, the created human being is endowed with the basic inclination to set out in search of the Absolute ("to seek God, and perhaps they might grope for him and find him", says Paul: Acts 17:27f.), so that when God in turn sets out in search of man in order to bestow grace upon him, he may not meet with indifference and unreceptivity. In revealed religion, therefore, natural religion is presupposed as a basis and included. Man's spontaneity toward God is needed. But henceforth it cannot act according to its own plans; rather, it is regulated by the grace freely encountering it and is thus protected from making itself absolute or becoming an inflexible "method". This human impoverishment in the area of methodical knowledge and of self-taught spiritual acrobatics is an enrichment in the gospel sense: "Happy the poor in spirit". Can one who has "mastered" the eight degrees of yoga really be called "poor" in spirit, however much he may be intent on becoming inwardly "empty"? Christian

156

training can aim only at increasingly perfect availability toward God and his will. Hence we shall
presently see that a (seeming) similarity in the
ways of Eastern and Western meditation does
exist, and that the ways, methods and practices
look so similar as to be mistaken for one another
and can even coincide materially (revealed religion
does not invalidate the religious element but fulfills it). But the more the specifically Christian
dimension comes to the fore, the more the specifically human constituent becomes manifest, and
this specificity has its repercussions—as one only
now fully recognizes—in the first apparently common steps.

a. Certainly we have in common a dedication
to exercises geared to essential freedom for the
Absolute: purification from exterior and interior
attachments; cutting the bonds of the passions that
shackle us to external things; gaining distance
from worldly fascinations; controlling the tongue,
and also the imagination and wandering thoughts;
relinquishing one's own personal interests as the
core around which everything revolves; concen-
trating the spiritual powers in one's inmost heart
("redire ad cor": Augustine), in which that silence
reigns which is the precondition for genuine,
spiritual seeing and hearing. The Spiritual Exercises also require this progressive disengagement

on the part of the exercitant in order to prepare him to "touch" God and receive his grace.[16] Here, however, we can already note a twofold difference:

1. For one who practices Eastern meditation (and for many Christian monks influenced by it, such as Evagrius Ponticus), the practice of love of neighbor (*praktikē*)—as an exercise in selflessness —is, as part of this preparatory purification, a *means to the end* of higher contemplation; whereas in an authentic Christian way, it can never sink to the level of a preliminary stage.

2. Someone who practices Eastern meditation will try from the outset to acquire a state of inner simplicity by abstraction from all objective thoughts, ideas and so forth; while in Christian meditation, one must never understand God's word of grace for which one readies oneself *solely* as an inner word, but always *also* as a word that comes to us in history and has become man. In this respect, the latter, compared to the former, would seem to be at a disadvantage. But this is the case only if one fails to understand Christian meditation for what it is from God's viewpoint: an exercise, by means of Christ's outward life, example and sacramental action, in inner knowledge and faith experience of what God is both for us and in himself. The apparently pure objectivity of a medi-

[16] N. 20.

tation on the life of Jesus, if it is to be meaningful in a Christian way, must lead beyond this objectification from the start, for the meditation should bring to light how the Absolute (God) *is*, for whose coming we are preparing ourselves in our entire (that is, principally in our truest) being. According to the Spiritual Exercises also, in letting ourselves be moved by an external scene, we are to become aware of "the infinite fragrance and sweetness of the divinity"[17] that becomes manifest through the scene. (We know that, for the Buddhist, Nirvana is also "perfumed".) For the Christian, withdrawal from the distracting exterior—recollection inwards—is only a means of ordering the *entire* person and never an end in itself; for since the God of the Bible, becoming incarnate, wants to be received in man's *entire* being and not merely in his inmost self, man's preparatory, purifying recollection must likewise have an effect on his whole physical, everyday existence.

b. Purification in the Christian sense is, above all, conversion to love, which is attained, not solely or even chiefly by means of methodical practice, but by accepting and passing on the forgiveness one has received from God. The reception of this forgiveness requires, not a state of nonreflective absorption, but one of *recollected*

[17] N. 124.

awareness, in which true contrition is aroused and any disorder in one's relationship to one's fellow-men can be put in order. According to the Sermon on the Mount, reconciliation with one's estranged brother is a prerequisite for one's (self-) offering in the (interior) temple. The Buddhist, too, certainly knows much about the ethical attitude of selflessness required of one who meditates. It is conditioned, however, by the theoretical knowledge that I and Thou (as also I and the Absolute) are ultimately not opposites, with the result that this ethical selflessness remains merely an aspect of the metaphysical selflessness of the meditator.[18] This is not to deny that "passive purifications" of the spirit really exist (as John of the Cross describes them); but they are undoubtedly always preceded by an active purification in the ordinary state of consciousness and are not a process methodically pursued by human effort.

c. For both East and West, the gathering of one's powers to center them in the simple "ground of the soul" can produce a similar consciousness of having transcended the subject–object duality. But this experience can be a preliminary stage of true openness for the Absolute, for God. It can be a self-contemplation of the subject, or the

[18] Henri de Lubac, *Aspects du Bouddhisme* (1950), vol. 1, "*La Charité bouddhique*", 11–53.

contemplation of the conditions for a possible objective contemplation, or contemplation of a cosmically expanded consciousness, or contemplation of oneself as image of God or of one's open longing for the Absolute.[19] Here we would also need to ask the Rheinland mystics what they ultimately meant by their ideal of the soul's nakedness: whether a de-objectification in the sense of Eastern meditation (which is not a supreme value from the Christian point of view), or elimination of all man's resistance to God—perfect, humble transparency (only this is a supreme value in the Christian sense). As a means, the practice of a de-objectifying form of meditation can contribute to such divesting, which permeates the Christian's whole existence; but it is neither to be confused nor equated with it. There certainly are other ways that God can use with a person, or that a person can take in his relationship with God, which lead to the same goal by different paths. The most perfect human word of consent—"Behold, I am the handmaid of the Lord; let it be done to me according to your word"—probably did not (since the speaker was a Jewess) mature through the practice of de-objectifying meditation.

In conclusion, let us state that the ambiguity of

[19] "Desiderium naturale": Karl Rahner in *Das mystische Wort*, viii–ix.

the word "selflessness"—in its Eastern and Western Christian accentuations—favors a commonality in the initial steps, whether understood from the ethical or the psychologico-metaphysical viewpoint. Just as the Buddhist has to let go of the illusion of his ego as a substantial center in order to catch sight of the Absolute, so must the Christian let go of the "geocentricity" of his self-awareness, in which everything revolves around his psychological ego, in favor of a heliocentric, that is, theocentric world view in which the self of creation and grace is received entirely from the central sun of divine grace and is determined by it. This divine center is so much the Absolute that the word "objective" in the worldly sense is not applicable to it. According to Augustine, it is at the same time "more inward to me than I am to myself and more exalted above me", and on this account it comes both from "within" and from "above and without". In this coming, the finite self is established, affirmed and loved by God, and not only my own self but that of every single person, each of whom in his essential uniqueness and irreplaceability is a reflection of the unique God and an increasingly better reflection the nearer he comes to God. Here, what is peculiar to Christian meditation in contrast to Eastern meditation becomes fully evident.

Generally speaking, the Christian remainder becomes evident in the fact that God's historical self-revelation in salvation history, climaxing in Christ, can never be relativized, surpassed or bracketed in an individual's encounter with God. In this self-revelation, God wanted to lay bare his inmost heart, for he loved the world so much that he gave his only-begotten Son for it. The Christian is invited and drawn into this salvation history objectively, whether he is aware of it or not—for example, in a state of absorption. He is needed for this history. We shall consider three aspects of this remainder that belong intrinsically together.

a. As called into being by God, the creaturely, free "I" is definitively prized, desired and loved; for God, it is a Thou. This free Thou was created concrete enough to receive God, for he wants to *become man* in his Son. In the Son, the image and likeness of God that man is becomes completely transparent to the prototype: "He who sees me sees the Father."[20] Therefore, as we have already said, genuine Christian meditation is not only "categorical" but "transcendental", or better—since here these categories are not adequately

[20] Jn 14:9.

applicable—sacramental. In Jesus the Good Shepherd, we see God the Good Shepherd;[21] Jesus is God's authentic, unsurpassable "interpretation".[22] In his apparently finite acts, sufferings and sentiments, the ever-Greater of the infinite God becomes manifest. Here we can perceive the role of "negative theology" within Christianity. Its task is not to negate every statement predicated of God, because the concept is always specified in content, while the Absolute, on the contrary, can be only the perfect absence of any specification. Instead, the task of negative theology is to indicate the plenitude that is revealed and contained in the finite "sacrament" and surpasses all our notions, being always more than what I could ever comprehend even by transcending myself to the utmost. (A necessary reflection of this Christian negativity is present in the Christian I–Thou relationship between persons: in true love, the Thou is loved in himself, and this self in his freedom is always more than his manifestations and any notion I may entertain regarding him.) Furthermore, the incarnate Son is he who, in the most absolute manner, receives from the Father and owes him everything; as such he will eternally say: "The Father is greater than I."[23] It does not occur to him to want to identify himself with

[21] Ez 31:11ff.
[22] Jn 1:18. [23] Jn 14:28.

the Father just because he is prefigured in the Father as his origin and therefore could take possession of his "exemplary identity" in him. Hence, in the Incarnation of the Son we are shown not only the exemplary attitude of the creature toward God but a prototypical attitude in God himself: to receive and to be indebted is itself divine and thus definitive.

b. Like the Buddhist, the Christian ponders the monstrous burden of suffering in the world, behind which is the burden of guilt. But for the Christian, this burden cannot be eliminated by means of meditation (as an unburdening), not even by means of the renowned "compassion" of the one who has become Buddha and renounces entering into Nirvana as long as there are suffering beings in the world. What happens on Golgotha is something totally different. It is a vicarious taking away of the world's guilt, solidarity in Godforsakenness, but out of love for those who have turned away from God, and thus their reconciliation. (At this point we cannot and need not develop the entire depths of the theology of the Cross.) One thing can be gathered from this: there is no Christian way to God, whether it be a "mystical" or any other way, that does not bear the stamp of what happened on the Cross. Practically nothing is said about this in the numerous Christian works about Zen meditation. Paul, caught up to the third heaven, bears the marks of Christ's wounds on his body. The "dark nights" of the mystics, if they are Christian and genuine, are by no means mere anthropological purifications of the ground of the soul in order to share better in the divine light; they are participations in Christ's Passion. Paul "fills up what is still lacking in Christ's sufferings".[24] He does not live as one passing from this world to a God who is above and beyond this world; he lives within God's involvement in behalf of the world, and this involvement means the Cross. Impelled by God and in union with Christ, he lets himself be put in the "last place"[25] for sinners and for the Church; and if God desired, he would be "separated from Christ" for the sake of his brethren.[26] Not the light of Tabor but the total darkness and the cry of abandonment on the Cross is the summit of Jesus' earthly existence. (In this regard, Saint Thérèse of Lisieux perhaps understood a bit more than even John of the Cross.)

c. Finally, the supreme Christian value is not the experience of transcendence but bearing the monotony of everyday life in faith, hope and love. As we mentioned in the beginning, the counterpart to the Eastern yogi or Zen master (who has attained the summit of human achievement) is

[24] Col 1:24.
[25] 1 Cor 4:9.   [26] Rom 9:3.

not the Christian mystic but the *Christian saint*, whether mystic or not. The saint knows asceticism as an exercise in perpetual presence before God: "Speak, Lord, your servant is listening."[27] Like the Eastern meditator, he too must recollect himself from worldly distraction and alienation and dig himself out of mundane agglomerations. Then in his state of concentration, what he receives is his *mission*, which he regards as foreseen for him by God: his mission coincides exactly with his own self-understanding. But mission sends me from God out to the world and to my fellowmen (perhaps to a particular activity, perhaps to a sharing in the Passion of the crucified Son: the so-called contemplative orders in particular find their place here).

A mission, especially a qualitatively "great" mission, is given in intimacy with God, in solitude, sometimes in ecstasy (as, for instance, the call of Isaiah or Jeremiah shows). If the mission is to succeed, the utmost selflessness and "indifferent" readiness for everything that God wants is required in this solitary encounter. In this total availability lies the true Christian analogy to the depersonalization of Eastern meditation. This "indifference" has to be preserved and to continue throughout

[27] 1 Sam 3:10.

the entire everyday mission and to be effective in all the spiritual powers of the one sent: his memory, understanding and will are "returned" to God, surrendered—as the Ignatian prayer of oblation has it—so that God alone may dispose of them. He always disposes, however, in favor of his world— which is why Christianity is the only religion that is really concerned with the world—and it is in this involvement with the world that God manifests his glory.

ARE THERE LAY PEOPLE
IN THE CHURCH?

Of course there are. This designation has established itself throughout the whole history of the Church. The particular constitutional law in the *Codex Iuris Canonici* has three headings: "Of Clerics", "Of Religious" and "Of Laity". So there can be no question of taking up arms against a time-honored concept that is deeply rooted in Christendom. The most we can do is reflect on its meaning and boundaries, and this in itself can have many consequences. Its boundaries are clear. They are drawn at the point where the cleric and the religious seem to have something that the lay person has not: an official consecration imparting powers that are not available to the layman, or a religious consecration initiating a form of personal Christian discipleship that is likewise closed to laypeople. The term "lay" has, of course, an utterly positive sense, since it comes from the word *laos*, that is, "(Church) people"; and it must be stressed that anyone who belongs to this "people", cleric and religious as well, is basically "lay"! At the same time, in general usage, its negative meaning preponderates: the lay person is a Christian believer who has neither the "privileges" of clerical office nor those of the religious state. As the secular usage of the word implies, such a person is the nonspecialist. Even in pagan antiquity the adjective *laikos* had this negative meaning, and in the Jewish context it meant a believer who was neither priest nor Levite.

This negative factor that excludes him from a certain sacral area necessarily places the lay person in a relationship to the profane, "secular" world; as this "world" acquires an increasingly positive value in the course of the Church's history (for the most varied reasons), this seems to enhance the lay person's chances of exercising a positive ecclesial role and vocation among the Church's many functions, without obliterating the other aspect we have already mentioned. The problems implicit here are increased by the difficulties inherent in the threefold division into "states" (*status, ordines vitae*), whereby a noncleric, i.e., a lay person, can still be a religious, with the result that the priest–lay axis is intersected by the religious–lay axis ("Christian in the world"). This difficulty is compounded in the case of members of "secular institutes", who wish to belong at the same time both to the state of the evangelical counsels (which religious vow to follow) and also to the lay state.

The only way out of this confusing situation is to reflect on the nature of ecclesial existence, indeed on the very nature of the Church, however risky such reflection may be. But it will be encompassed by the simple truth that every Christian in the Church is called and drawn equally to perfection in the love of God and love of neighbor, or—which is the same thing—that there are diverse gifts of grace, offices and ways of serving in the Church, but only one Spirit, one Lord, one God (1 Cor 12:4–6).

1.

In Jesus the "kingdom of heaven" has come near to earth, that eschatological reality to which the beatitudes and the apparently utopian guidelines of the Sermon on the Mount refer; the call to repentance goes forth, and the invitation to believe the saving message (Mk 1:5). But this is still a long way from Church structure. True, in God's redemptive plan, the beloved Son will be delivered into the hands of sinners and will die for them, but he by no means begins with the proclamation of this final phase of his destiny. He begins, in fact, with the free, almost paradisiacally, naive offer of the attitude of his heavenly Father: Be perfect, be merciful, as your Father in heaven is perfect and merciful (Mt 5:8; Lk 6:36). His heart knows no violence: "Turn the other cheek"; it does not seek its own: "Be not anxious about tomorrow"; it does not keep old scores: "As we forgive our debtors". Will this kingdom, with its heavenly attitudes, be able to gain a foothold on the earth? Jesus does not abrogate the law, but in the same breath he demands an attitude "far more perfect than that of the scribes and Pharisees", something that, even formally, is far above the law (as it was understood in the Old Covenant). For the latter was only for the "lawless and disobedient" (1 Tim 1:9), whereas the person who lives in the manner of the kingdom of heaven fulfills all laws as if incidentally (Rom 13:8–10). Who can live like this? Even before setting out this program in his preaching, however, Jesus called by name a clearly defined group of individuals. He demanded that they put their whole life in his hands (they "left everything and followed him") and entrusted the words of the kingdom to them, even giving them "authority" to drive back the spirit at enmity with God in the face of the approaching Holy Spirit (Mk 3:13–15). In Jesus, the kingdom of heaven takes root on earth in such a way that a seed of community is formed at the same time; it is to this community that the Sermon on the Mount is addressed (Mt 5:2), while the crowd listens.

We are still a long way from the foundation of a hierarchy. We have two things: first, the demand (and its fulfillment) for a radical discipleship, in terms of daily existence, for the sake of the kingdom and lived according to its customs; second, together with Jesus, the disciples are authorized and shortly thereafter sent out to proclaim and initiate this kingdom. Everything will develop from this center: later, the specific powers of ministry; later still, the organization of a particular form of life of "leaving everything". (The latter will involve a withdrawal from the world; but only half of the original community correspond to this movement.) Above all it will involve that spiritual radicalism (striking root in the kingdom of heaven) which will be demanded of every Christian on being admitted into the Church. Here it appears as an "incarnate" forsaking of everything (one could say "literal" forsaking, but it is too narrow a term for something which is primarily a matter of the "spirit"). If one looks for a way of life in the developed Church which approximates this original form, one might think of the "secular institutes", whose members follow the radicalism of the counsels but do not wish to live separated from the world, and may or may not be priests. But even these communities already have an institution according to canon law; this was not present in the fluidity of the Church's beginnings. This early way of life can certainly not be limited to a state that excluded women; it is precisely women whom we see accompanying the Lord and ministering to him.

It is most important to see that the kingdom that has come near from the Father in the person of Jesus cannot be cramped within forms that belong to a human society alienated from God, whether they are profane or sacral forms. Just as the Risen Lord (in his body) walks through locked doors, so from the first the embodiment of the kingdom moves through closed organizations. The Church has continually striven toward this origin, which, although it belongs to the first phase of the Incarnation of the divine, still remains "u-topian" ("The Son of Man has nowhere . . .": *ouk echei pou*, Mt 8:20). Jesus' state of displacement at the beginning of his mission has been compared to Francis, for instance, whose ideal is above any rule of life livable on earth, an ideal that must first "die", losing itself in a particular form or in various forms through which the ideal can once again be striven for. What Ignatius originally had in mind—before the Inquisition obliged him to study theology—belongs in this category also.

2.

Loisy's remark that the kingdom was proclaimed but the Church arrived is true, but in a wholly different sense than he intended. Jesus proclaims the kingdom as a genuine possibility, seen from the vantage point of heaven; from the viewpoint of sinful earth, however, of Israel, "who murders the prophets", it seems impossible. As, externally, the fate of Jesus moves toward suffering, as it becomes apparent that, in the total plan of the triune God, the kingdom can gain a foothold on earth only through the Cross and Resurrection, we begin to discern the outlines of that form of the Church which is marked by the event of the Cross and Resurrection. As Jesus' silent obedience to the Father becomes a hard obedience through his acceptance of the burden of sin, as the Holy Spirit above him hardens into an objective, pitiless Rule, and as, on the other hand, his flesh and blood become Eucharist through the winepress of the Cross, to be directly accessible to those who come after, the original mode of discipleship is complemented by ecclesial office. From now on this office will be located at the intersection of two spheres, the sphere of the sinless Lord in his Passion and the sphere of sin, involving a total interpenetration that completes the movement of Incarnation in the full realism of our world as it is. The authority of the hierarchy has its origin in the Cross, although it is to be exercised and obeyed in the Holy Spirit of the Risen Christ. Similarly, dying to the world and obedience, two things that characterize the life of the counsels, now acquire features of the Passion which, again, can be lived only in the Spirit of Easter. Finally, the whole Christian life is drawn into the rhythm of death and resurrection, as Paul shows in Romans 6: in baptism, at the very outset, we are configured to the dying and buried Lord; having descended with him, we can ascend with him to a sinless risen life for God.

In distinguishing two phases of Jesus' procla-mation of the kingdom, we are simply following the scheme of the Gospels, which in the scene at Caesarea Philippi illustrate a watershed in the life of Jesus: the beginning of the prophecies of his

175

suffering and of the journey to Jerusalem. We are in no way implying that Jesus only realized late in the day that he would have to suffer. The great prophets were told at the very time of their call and commissioning that their mission would fail. Jesus may well have devoted all his energy to proclaiming the kingdom as his Father wished, all the time entrusting to his Father the knowledge that it would fail. Eventually the theme of the Cross became a reality, requiring appropriate changes—concrete discipleship in the light of the Cross!—in the community of his followers.

The objectivity of official authority is required so that Jesus' central "hour" in which he bears the world's sin on the Cross, merging (timelessly) into the Resurrection, can remain a present reality for subsequent believers. But however necessary this element of infallible objectivity is—the un-worthiness of the office-bearer aside—existentially it cannot be divorced from the first call to follow Jesus. When Peter finally receives his office of feeding Jesus' lambs, two things happen: he is ob-liged to confess his "greater" love (in the presence of the "disciple whom Jesus loved"!: Jn 21:15), and the manner of his death is foretold him, that is, his configuration (which is also subjective) to the Good Shepherd who gives his life for the sheep:

176

"Follow me" (Jn 21:18f.). Office and authority are not torn out of the original matrix of the proclamation of the kingdom, which Jesus did not take up without the help of fellow messengers of whom he demanded an "incarnate forsaking of everything".

There is an inner convergence between New Testament priesthood and what has crystallized, with increasing clarity of form, as the state of the counsels. Considered in the abstract, the element of official objectivity has often, certainly, relegated this convergence to the background (in the pastoral epistles we find mention of married office-bearers). But, in his own life, Paul did not cease to insist with all possible emphasis that this convergence was right and fitting: he wields objective and subjective authority at the same time; he has the Lord's authority, yet can make himself the *typos* for the community, because he is a copy of Christ in his whole existence. And it is important to note that he does not break off his relationships with the working world: he remains a tentmaker in spite of the fact that he would be entitled to be supported by the communities. He lives as an official minister of Christ, but in evangelical poverty—which he does not interpret in the sense of a flight from the world. And of course he lives as a virgin, doubtless in imitation of the Lord, who lived eschatologically, only for his good news of the kingdom.

3.

This incarnate discipleship that later developed into life according to the evangelical counsels (we cannot go into the many ramifications of its history here) can best be characterized by the concept "radicalism". This radicalism means that incarnate discipleship, "forsaking everything", can move forward into the situation of Cross and Resurrection: into the unconditionality of a pneumatic obedience to a rule that is inspired by the Spirit but given a personal interpretation through a superior; into the unconditionality of a death to the world that is anchored totally in the death of Christ and not in Neoplatonic flight from the world. It must be admitted that alien ideology has often been taken as an expression of genuinely Christian truths and values here, but it does not call the latter's foundation into question. To die to the world (as every Christian must do, in conscious affirmation, at baptism) does not mean to flee from the world. To die to the world in Christ means to give oneself, along with Christ, for the world and for its benefit—another point which was pushed too far into the background in official monastic theology. Where it is truly lived, the incarnational radicalism of the counsels is apostolic of its very nature, in accordance with the dictum about the grain of wheat falling into the ground and dying and thus bringing forth much fruit.

By being drawn into the radicalism of the Cross and there taking on objectivized forms, the life of the counsels retains a particular relation to the initial mode of proclamation of the kingdom: namely, it is counselled but not commanded. The inner form of Jesus' program was God's "counsel", God's "will", even when it seemed that he was tightening the "commandments" of the Old Covenant: "It has been said—but I say to you." The logic of the new, evangelical perfection is not a "must", but a "may". But this "may", if it is to prove and perfect itself in discipleship of the Son, must be transposed into the iron "must" (the *dei* of salvation history: "Christ had to suffer"). Indeed, this christological "must" is, for the disciple, the highest and most gracious "may".

Insofar as the "counsel" is one aspect of New Testament love as a whole, it concerns every Christian. It is a question of Christ's individual call and choice whether a person may and ought to give this general Christian "life of the counsels" the particular pattern that, in the history of the

Church, has taken on the form of professing vows. It is the purpose of the Exercises to ascertain whether a person is hearing Christ's special call choosing him to follow "actual poverty (etc.)" or whether, as a Christian striving equally for perfection, he is called to "spiritual poverty (etc.)" (*Exercises*, no. 98). Since the particular election is a matter for the Lord, and it is not up to the Christian to choose the "more perfect" path for himself according to some theoretical rule, there is no injustice if he is not chosen for the "actual" life of the counsels. Rather he must consider two things: that this mode of life belongs only *instrumentaliter et dispositive* to perfection (St. Thomas, *S. Th.* II/II 186, 2), and that, consequently, the endeavor to follow Christ completely by keeping the command of love can certainly "lead to Christian perfection" (*Exercises*, no. 135).

4.

Now we can proceed to speak of Christians who are usually termed "laity", in the negative sense that they are part neither of the official priesthood nor of the incarnate life of the counsels, although —and this is the positive sense—they are full members of the community of the Church.

A more precise explanation is needed here, however: the relation of laypeople both to those bearing office and those living the counsels is not a cut-and-dried matter but an analogy. This analogy as such is grounded in an identical vocation to the life of the Church and to the radicalism of a love that is centered in Christ.

The analogy between the "lay" person and the bearer of office lies in their different relationships to the one "universal priesthood" of all Christians: the whole Christ, head and body, offers to God the total surrender of himself, the true spiritual sacrifice that is pleasing to God and enables him to be reconciled with the sinful world (cf. Augustine, *Civ. Dei* X, 6). Just as every one of the baptized enters into the death of Christ, so everyone does likewise who assists at the eucharistic celebration by being prepared to offer himself together with Christ in the Church's gifts of bread and wine at the offertory. If he is prepared to surrender (to "sacrifice") his most precious possession—his Lord and Savior—for the salvation of the world, how much more his own self, which is as nothing in comparison! *"Meum ac vestrum sacrificium"*, says the priest to the congregation; but the analogy here is rooted in a common *"nostrum"* which becomes indistinguishable in Christ's self-sacrifice. The same analogy announces itself in the different relation of each state of life to the office of proclamation. The priest's task is primarily to proclaim and interpret the teaching of the gospel to the believers and to bear witness to it by his whole life (here the pastoral office becomes involved), whereas the lay person extends this proclamation into the world by transmitting the testimony of the truth, received in the Church, to the non-Christian environment outside, by his example and by giving an account of the faith that is in him (1 Pet 3:15). The notion that mission is chiefly a matter for the clergy must be seriously questioned. Neither Scripture nor Church history supports that view, nor, in particular, does the present state of Christendom. Think, for example, of Péguy's call: "We are all in the front line" (Laudet, 82–87). With regard to the pastoral office, it is primarily a function within the Church serving the whole ecclesial community (not least its unity in spirit and faith); it is only a witness to Christ *ad extra*, as a result of this primary activity and the use Christians make of it. If Christians as a body did not supply the witness to unity that a function like that of the Papacy is designed to promote, such a function would be in vain. Here, too, the inner analogy comes to light again, leaving aside the delicate problem of the acceptance of the hierarchy's decisions by the faithful (*réception*).

We have already discussed the analogy between laity and people living the counsels when we spoke of Christ's freedom to call "those whom he will" (Mk 3:13), both men and women, into a closer discipleship. No one who has not received this call can complain that the Lord has relegated him to second place. It must be remembered that the disciples in the Gospel were called during the first phase of its proclamation, at a time when the differentiation of "states" in the Church had not yet developed. All were summoned to enter into the sphere of the kingdom, meaning the perfect spirit of the divine Father's love, which was now to make its home on earth. The call to the kingdom is the radicalism that embraces all forms of Christian life. It would be wrong to designate religious life and lay life respectively as the "state of the counsels" and the "state of the command-ments", for the commandments of the Old Testa-ment are transcended in the sphere of "counsel", of doing "more" in spontaneity, because the God now being revealed is the God who is always more, always greater.

With this as their origin, all Christians are first of all simply Christians. All have to strive from now on for the "more" of this new love. This picture is presented in John's epistles, for instance, where there is no mention of states or forms of life. But the same thing can be found even in the letters of Paul, in which the figure of the Apostle as the preeminent hierarch and exemplar of the counsels emerges so strongly: the community is continually being challenged to share in everything that the Apostle does, suffers and plans. The "I" is for ever being changed involuntarily into a "we"; Paul's "I" ultimately sees itself simply as "your servant".

5.

A brief word on marriage, which is a possible (but not a necessary) form of "lay" life, contrary to the life of the counsels and closed to clergy of the Western Church (because of the convergence we noted between office and special election). Marriage does not cross the threshold of the eschatological realm (Mt 22:30), and a person who wishes to live eschatologically should therefore renounce marriage if he can (Mt 19:12; 1 Cor 7:8f.). Yet marriage, which was originally instituted by God (Mk 10:6; Eph 5:31), may not be represented as un-Christian and simply obsolete (1 Tim 4:3); in many situations it is urgently recommended (1 Tim 5:14; 1 Cor 7:9). But in the New Testament the ideality of marriage is not to be found in marriage itself but in the suprasexual relationship between Christ and the Church: as a sacrament, it participates in this relationship by orienting itself toward the "great mystery" (Eph 5:32), striving

184

toward and molding itself on it. Although (as Augustine explicitly says) the virgin is not as such more perfect than the married person, virginity as such *is* more perfect than the married life:[1] in virginity vowed for the love of Christ, the "form" is perfect and life must be fashioned in accordance with it as far as possible, whereas in marriage the "form" is still imprisoned in the old era, and a great effort is needed to refine the earthly *eros* so that it may become a pure expression of heavenly *agape*. By the power of Christ's grace, and sacramental grace in particular, this effort can achieve its goal, but not without many renunciations, which lead, again, from the sphere of the proclamation of the gospel to that of the Cross.

6.

Finally, everything in the Church that bears the mark of a special, qualitative election (clerical office or the "counsels") is subject to the dialectic of the "last place" so insisted upon by Jesus and Paul. For if he whom we rightly call Lord and Master chooses the "last place" (Jn 13:13), those

---

[1] "Si quis dixerit, statum coniugalem anteponendum esse statui virginitatis vel caelibatus et non esse melius ac beatius manere in virginitate aut caelibatu quam iungi matrimonio: Anathema sit." *Conc. Trid.*, ses. 24, can. 10.

who are his "servants" and "those who are sent" must do the same. Everything that is structured in the Church is ministry; consequently, whatever is not part of that (qualitative) structure is given the (dangerous!) first place: "For all things are yours, whether Paul or Apollos or Cephas or the world or life or death or the present or the future, all are yours", if "you are Christ's, and Christ is God's" (1 Cor 3:21b–23). Christians of the local community form the core of the Church; clerical office ministers to them, and the life of the counsels acts as fertilizer, "dung" (Augustine). Seen in this way, the negative aspect of the term "lay" disappears completely, and the word can be simply replaced by "Christian". If the bearer of office is an "ambassador" (2 Cor 5:20) to the community with an ever-new message from Christ, a "steward" of his mysteries (1 Cor 4:1), this embassy in and to the Church is directed toward an embassy to the world on the part of the whole Church, both the concrete community and every individual: thus even the Christian who receives an ambassador of Christ becomes an ambassador in his turn, furnished with a personal charism that is never a goal in itself but always the means to some service to be performed. It cannot be made equivalent (quantitatively, by degrees) to the apostolic office (in such a way that the community itself would ultimately govern the office), but this charism means that all are one body with many members: "You have one teacher, and you are all brethren" (Mt 23:8).

WOMEN PRIESTS?

The worldwide offensive of "feminism", which is battling for the equality of women with men, takes effect within the Church as the women's claim to the ministerial priesthood. As a whole, the battlefront presents a confusing picture, and this in turn affects the ecclesial arena, which in addition has its own special problems.

1.

On the whole, the assault of "feminism" is in a fatal predicament, because it is fighting for equal rights for women in a predominantly male-oriented, technological civilization. Thus it either takes up the front against this civilization as such (or, what amounts to about the same thing, against the masculinity shaping it) or claims its place within this civilization, which can scarcely be done without an unnatural masculinization of woman or a levelling of the difference between the sexes. All these possibilities contain a priori a contradiction more or less perceptible in the parlance and program of the movement. This contradiction, however, may by no means be dismissed as "feminine illogic"; rather, it conceals a profound tragedy of our times.

The era of matriarchal culture has long since come to an end, and that of patriarchal culture is likewise over, though not so long since. We are living in a time both fatherless and motherless, and it is anachronistic to characterize and approach our modern forms of society on the basis of an obsolete patriarchy. The natural relationship between the typical male outlook and mankind's present (and probably, future) technologized way of life has nothing to do with a dominance of the father in the clan; rather, it is traceable to the prevalence of a rationalism to which natural things and conditions mean above all material for manufacturables. Of course, as long as culture has existed, man has also been *homo faber*; but as long as there really was *culture*, man retained his balance in an attitude that contemplated nature while being receptive to its essence, an attitude that we can in general term philosophical. When philosophy

188

ends where the contemplative-receptive glance has turned into a merely calculating one (what one can do with a thing), a feminine element—to state it briefly—that makes a person *secure* in nature and in being is abandoned in favor of a preponderance of the masculine element, which pushes forward into things in order to change them by implanting and imposing something of its own.

The sexual image suggested here should not be pressed, for the philosophical attitude of letting oneself be gifted and fructified by nature and being is not feminine in the sense of mere receptivity. A forward-moving way of thinking certainly reigns in this attitude: one, of course, which, like the fructified womb, is able to bear patiently the seeds received and give birth to them in images, myths and concepts. In the contemplating intellect, the active element of the feminine principle is wedded to the passive element of the masculine (which needs the self-bestowing womb in order to be able to give) in the best possible way. On the contrary, where positivistic, technology-oriented thinking succeeds in reigning supreme, the female element also vanishes from the attitude of the man. There is no longer anything that maternally embraces the human being's existence; under the power of the human spirit, nature has descended to the level of mere material; even the spirit itself is in danger

189

of becoming material for self-manipulation, and being as a whole, as unreifiable, is overlooked.

This epochal forgetting, in which the femininity of the woman is also forgotten, cannot be reversed by any kind of rationally expedient planning, least of all by the woman's moving into the already overpopulated other side. Such a change would totally destroy the disturbed balance, level the all-fructifying difference between the sexes in favor of an asexuality (with male indications, however) and consume humanity's last ideological reserves. For, evidently, a humanity devoid of philosophy and victim to the pure positivism of "making"—and in the end of self-making—is without norms and thus without direction. And if a great part of this technological civilization is running itself idly to death anyway, there is some hope only because another part—today, in addition to some prudent women, this comprises above all young people who eye the prevalent activism with mistrust—is creating reserves that will assure survival after the downfalls: reserves that are not geared to "needs" and "consumption", like everything about which we are worried (the economy, the Third World, ecological preservation), but to being, to the background that gives meaning to things, to security, to making a home for man who is always on the run, exposed to the world—all of which is essentially the woman's role.

At such a late hour of history, can we still hope for a return of this sense-giving balance—which is only symbolically intimated in the sexual, but in reality extends much farther and concerns the human being in his place within being as a whole? If we can do so, then certainly only through the woman who perceives and understands her role as counterpoise to and spearhead against man's increasingly history-less world, and then must do just the opposite of what current feminism does. Neither competition with man in the typically masculine field nor a rationally drawn up (with masculine means!) counteraction against the masculine world is meaningful; meaning can be found only in creating a vital force against history-less, technologized existence, in abstaining from the artificial superabundance being offered with a view to noticing anew the real "superabundance of life". We must not imagine that things will fall into place by themselves; it would take deep moral decisions on the part of women to seize the spokes of the wheel that is rolling toward the absurd. . . .

2.

Over against the old world, whose balance is so endangered, the Church is the beginning of the new cosmos founded in Jesus Christ. In that new cosmos, from its very foundation, the right balance, including sexual balance, is assured. It is only a matter of recognizing it and living in it. The Church begins with the Yes of the Virgin of Nazareth, which summarizes Israel's faith and brings it to abundant fulfillment: unreserved readiness to conceive, in full freedom, making woman's entire psychophysical fruitfulness available. It is an active fruitfulness, incredibly surpassing all the natural fruitfulness of the woman, which is already superior to that of the man; and it carries, brings forth, nurtures and educates, not just any child, but God's Son. Just as he owes what he is to his eternal Father, so too he owes it to this motherly, ecclesial womb; and he will gradually educate Mary—pierced by the sword—unto the Cross, where he will consecrate her as the mother of his disciple, of the Apostles and of the visible ecclesial assembly.

The Twelve whom he commissions and invests with the necessary powers are chosen thirty years later. They receive masculine tasks of leadership and representation within the comprehensive feminine, marian Church. They begin as failures—this is demonstrated most clearly in the case of Peter—and can never match the quality of the primordial Church, the "perfect Bride", the *Immaculata*. Their role is a service within the permanent existence of the Church: they are to represent him who, by virtue of the surrender of his entire substance on the Cross, gathers the people of God into himself eucharistically and places it under the Father's great absolution. In view of his self-giving (by no means in view of any act of Peter), Christ's "pre-redeemed" Mother has also received the grace to speak her impeccable, infallible Yes. What Peter will receive as "infallibility" for his office of governing will be a partial share in the total flawlessness of the feminine, marian Church. And what the men, consecrated into their office, receive in the way of power to consecrate and to absolve will again be in its specifically masculine function—the *transmission* of a vital force that originates outside itself and leads beyond itself—a share in a fruitfulness (before the Eucharist, she gave birth to Christ) and purity (she was absolved from all eternity) belonging nonofficially to the perfect feminine Church.

One can say that Christ, inasmuch as he represents the God of the universe in the world, is likewise the origin of both the feminine and masculine principles in the Church; in view of him, Mary is pre-redeemed, and Peter and the Apostles are installed in their office. And insofar as Christ is a man, he again represents the origin, the Father, for the fruitfulness of the woman is always dependent on an original fructification. Neither of these points is to be relativized, nor is the resultant representation of the origin by the Church's office.

A woman who would aspire to this office would be aspiring to specifically masculine functions, while forgetting the precedence of the feminine aspect of the Church over the masculine. With this ecclesial feminism we again arrive at the sphere of what we described in the first section, in which the woman, through a tragic misunderstanding, reaches for what is specifically masculine; except that now it is considerably easier to rectify. The right balance need not be arduously sought, for it is already present in the essence of the Church. In order to perceive this, of course, one must have an eye for the fundamental marian dimension of the Church, the eye possessed by the Church Fathers, the Middle Ages and even the baroque period and lost only by us—during the period of the rationalistic Enlightenment. The title "Mother of the Church" represents an attempt to recapture something of the awareness belonging to Christianity for nearly two thousand years. But in this awareness, "Mother" and "Church" were even more closely joined: in the image of the "mantle of grace" for instance, the Church's prototype and the universal Church living within her ambit flow into one another.

If one takes an unbiased stance, one has to marvel at how intensely this prototype, precisely in recent times, by means of active testimonies from heaven, has been offered to the world as a reminder and a point of reflection. From Catherine Labouré to Bernadette at Lourdes, to Beauraing, Banneux and Fatima (to mention only important and recognized instances), the self-testimony of the *Ecclesia immaculata* is uninterrupted. She is not allowed to hide herself behind her Son in false humility; she comes uninhibitedly to the fore and manifests her nature: "I am the Immaculate Conception", she insists at Lourdes, and this in connection with the Rosary, which points clearly enough to the divine origin of the Son and of the entire Trinity. The masculine hierarchy was willing enough to recognize the messages of Lourdes and Fatima, and the numerous marian encyclicals of the popes have underscored the rightful place of woman in the Church's inmost nature.

Because of her unique stucture, the Catholic Church is perhaps humanity's last bulwark of genuine appreciation of the difference between the sexes. In the dogma of the Trinity, the Persons must be equal in dignity in order to safeguard the distinction that makes the triune God subsistent love; in a similar way, the Church stresses the equal dignity of man and woman, so that the extreme oppositeness of their functions may guarantee the spiritual and physical fruitfulness of human nature. Every encroachment of one sex into the role of the other narrows the range and dynamics of humanly possible love, even when this range transcends the sphere of sexuality, birth and death and achieves the level of the virginal relationship between Christ and his Church, a relationship expressed, not in isolated individual acts of specific organs, but in the total surrender of one's own being.

The Church's marian dimension embraces the petrine dimension, without claiming it as its own. Mary is "Queen of the Apostles" without claiming apostolic powers for herself. She possesses something else and something more.

But modern man, who tries to make [machen] something out of every object, can only with difficulty distinguish between authority [Vollmacht] such as Jesus bestows and power [macht]. The two are, however, basically different. Ecclesial authority is a specific qualification for service to the community. It is appropriation as expropriation; leadership, but from the last place. One must, therefore, guard against exalting the service of the bishop and the priest to a quality fundamentally inaccessible to women. Like all Christians, women possess this quality eminently in the "universal priesthood" of all the faithful, which allows and basically effects an offering and being-offered of all together with Christ. (In this connection, Cardinal Mercier sowed confusion by proclaiming that the diocesan clergy is *the* state of perfection.) "Power" is so often unobtrusively behind many contestations and movements, supposedly in behalf of justice, equality and so forth, that, precisely in the case of the theme under consideration here, extreme caution and the most precise discernment of spirits are necessary. Both sexes, each in its own way, aspire to "power", and use the most varied methods to gain it. Power is connected subterraneously with humanity's original sin and concupiscence and, naturally, also makes itself felt as a motive within the Church. It is by no means a prerogative of men.

On the other hand, the ecclesial office, whose contour comes so expressly to the fore in the New Testament and from the earliest tradition onwards, may not be leveled into the other services and charisms in such a way that it appears merely as one single function among others: there is only one "shepherd" of the pastured flock, and this image remains valid even though so many single functions in a community are distributed among lay people, both women and men.

Who has precedence in the end? The man bearing office, inasmuch as he represents Christ in and before the community, or the woman, in whom the nature of the Church is embodied—so much

197

so that every member of the Church, even the priest, must maintain a feminine receptivity to the Lord of the Church? This question is completely idle, for the difference ought only to serve the mutual love of all the members in a circulation over which God alone remains sublimely supreme: "In the Lord, the woman is not independent of the man nor the man of the woman. For just as the woman [Eve] comes from the man, so also the man [including Christ] comes through the woman; but everything comes from God" (1 Cor 11:11–12).

A NOTE ON LAY THEOLOGIANS

Distinctions

The increasing number of laymen wanting to take up the study of theology without wishing to become priests is both heartening and disquieting, for two reasons. First, because in this way theology becomes one field of study among others; one can go to lectures in theology as well as other

198

subjects, and theology is thus only part of one's career (e.g., as a teacher). Knowing "about" God ("theo-logy") seems an accessory to expert knowledge about chemistry or English literature. This may present no problems for genuine lay-people pursuing a genuine life of faith and wishing to represent the Church in their work or home. By their subjective attitude of faith they can compensate for the unfortunate fact that Christian theology seems thus to be put at the same level as the secular subjects; they can change this "neutral" knowledge into something that is lived out in existential fashion.

But in this veritable flood of laymen there are a considerable number who in reality have a vocation to the priesthood but hold back in fear for a hundred secondary reasons—a passing inability to make up their mind, weakness of faith, worries about celibacy and so forth. In order to stifle their vocation, whether it is clearly or hazily perceived, they listen eagerly to the slogans trumpeted on all sides: "increasing secularization", "urgent need for the lay apostolate", "universal priesthood", "ministry as 'one' charism", "decentralization of the hierarchy", "democratization of Church structures" and so on. It is precisely this kind of traffic in slogans that makes these pseudo-laymen suspect and often easily recognized. While genuine laypeople carry out their role naturally in their particular situation—a really indispensable role, today more than ever—the "exaggerated" laymen feel compelled continually to stress their lay status and bolster it up theologically. They do this with such rhetoric and on such a broad front that one comes to accept their arguments as a sociological phenomenon that must be accounted for in the modern Church—especially as they (wrongly) claim to justify their actions on the basis of the Second Vatican Council. It is possible to detect a deep, poorly disguised resentment against the priestly office in the methods of unmasking that they like to employ. It must be said that discernment of spirits is made more difficult by the fact that the clergy themselves often speak in a similar manner, in order to seem *au courant*.

A Fallacy

An argument especially favored by these exaggerated laymen tries to demonstrate that almost all the functions regarded as specifically sacerdotal until now can also be exercised by laypeople and *are* actually done by them: religious education, preaching, administering Holy Communion, and so forth. The office of priest seems like a citadel that has been stormed repeatedly, and of which

only two towers remain: the power to give absolution and the power to speak the words of
consecration. If these are the only things that
distinguish the ordained priest from the Church's
other ministers, his office is reduced to the level of
the other ministries or offices, raising the serious
question as to whether it is meaningful to make
such a fuss about this difference. Why cannot a
member of the "universal priesthood" exercise
this special ministry for example in an emergency?
More pressingly still, why should the Church in
this case require the extraordinary resolution to
celibacy?

But this picture of a division of powers, whereby the priest retains only some, is misleading. The
priest is the principle of unity in the community,
as the bishop is for the diocese and the Pope for the
whole Church. Of course, they only *represent* a
unity that exists hidden in Jesus Christ. But they
represent it in virtue of a real power granted by
Christ. Only within the unity he gives can the
assembled community regard itself as one in Christ
and, on the basis of that oneness, divide into its
individual ministries and charisms. The image
of the shepherd that runs through the Scriptures
shows this clearly. The shepherd cannot be dis-
membered or replaced by sheep; he is not a func-
tionary (an employee, clerk or mercenary), but
the person responsible for the flock with his whole

existence. This is also the justification for celibacy: being a priest is not a "job" but the investment of one's whole life, as is clearly shown by the New Testament's demand (at all levels) for total commitment. Celibacy is to this extent more than a mere symbol of the community's oneness: together with the life commitment of Christ the Shepherd, it ensures that this oneness will be built up efficiently.

(In the Orthodox Church only the "lower" clergy are married; in the episcopate there is a convergence of priesthood and monasticism. To get an idea of what the Catholic Church with a largely noncelibate clergy would be like, one should read idyllic-ironic English novels like Trollope's *Barchester Towers*. If Catholic *viri probati* should ever be ordained, the truly "pastoral" functions would doubtless remain with the clergy living the evangelical counsels, on the basis of people's instinctual feeling.)

A Qualification

What I have said about lay theologians refers above all to men. Women do not experience a clear call to the priestly office, except perhaps in imagination. They can succumb to the previously mentioned danger, that of seeing theology demoted to one subject among the other secular disciplines; they are also frequently susceptible to the slogans of the lay ideology. But they are often more convincing helpers in pastoral care than any male "pastoral assistants".

Ought one to add that in many ways they often have a better understanding of total commitment and are in this sense nearer to the primary demand of the gospel? If one looks more closely it can be argued[1] that the first vocation is the vocation to unqualified discipleship (to leave everything, even one's wife and child: Lk 18:29), i.e., to that form of life which was later given the ecclesial structure of the religious life and to which women can be called as well as men, whereas the priesthood of the New Testament does not come into force until later, in connection with Christ's Passion (Eucharist) and Resurrection (Absolution). Finally, the Church as Mary's assent comes on the scene much earlier than the Church of the Twelve.

[1] This thesis cannot be developed here. See my book *Christlicher Stand* (Einsiedeln: Johannes Verlag, 1977 [Eng. ed. *The Christian State of Life* (San Francisco: Ignatius, 1983)]), and the brief essay above, "Are There Lay People in the Church?"

A WORD ON "HUMANAE VITAE"

I should like to offer a short meditation on the famous passage in the Letter to the Ephesians where Paul speaks of husband and wife and compares their relationship with the great mystery in which it is set, the mystery of the relationship of Christ to his Church. The passage is cited in *Humanae Vitae* but is not commented on there at any length. Naturally this passage, taken by itself, cannot substantiate every doctrine and every demand contained in that encyclical; and yet, if we meditate deeply on Paul's words, we may come to perceive some of the central truths of the encyclical in a fuller light. Of course this meditation makes no pretense to exact exegesis of the text; many points in it are still very much in debate. But first we should look at the text itself.

> Submit to one another in the fear of Christ. Wives should be submissive to their husbands as if to the Lord, because the husband is head of his wife just as Christ is head of his body the Church, as well as its savior. As the Church submits to Christ, so wives should submit to their husbands in everything.
>
> Husbands, love your wives, as Christ loved the Church. He gave himself up for her to make her holy, purifying her in the bath of water by the

power of the word, to present to himself a glorious Church, holy and immaculate, without stain or wrinkle or anything of that sort.

Husbands should love their wives as they do their own bodies. He who loves his wife loves himself. Observe that no one ever hates his own flesh; no, he nourishes it and takes care of it as Christ cares for the Church—for we are members of his body.

"For this reason a man shall leave his father and mother, and shall cling to his wife, and the two shall be made into one flesh."

This is a great mystery; I mean with reference to Christ and the Church.

In any case, each one should love his wife as he loves himself, the wife for her part showing respect for her husband.

The basic meaning is perfectly clear. Paul, or whoever the author may be—certainly someone close to Paul—is speaking here of Christian marriage, and he demands that Christian marriage be an unconditional following of Christ. He does not mean here that the two partners, as individual Christians, must each follow Christ; he makes it very clear that their marriage itself is to be a reflection of the relationship between Christ and the Church. These two relationships, man to woman, Christ to the Church, are closely intertwined, although (as we shall see) the place of Christ remains altogether unique and supreme. In marriage, as in all other human situations, Christ is our model, but a model to be *imitated*, not a model that can ever be duplicated.

Think of the hymn in Philippians. We are all to have the mind of Christ, who, though he was in the form of God, emptied himself, taking the form of man, and humbled himself even to death on the Cross. And for this reason God has exalted him above all creation and made him Lord of all. Now, we cannot imitate Christ in these things: we cannot empty ourselves of the form of God, or die on the Cross, or be exalted above all creation. But, Paul tells us, we must have the mind of Christ. And we can have a mind by which each of us "thinks of others, in humility, as superior to himself" and makes himself "concerned with others' interests, not with his own" (Phil 2:3).

So, too, Christian marriage can take its structure from the relationship between Christ and the Church, even though that relationship presents an archetype that marriage can never perfectly resemble. Yet marriage can be lived psychologically within the rhythm of Christ's relations with the Church, because in truth and reality Christian marriage *exists* only within the sphere of influence of the archetypical marriage of Christ with his Church. At the end of our text Paul adds: "This is a great mystery; I mean with reference to Christ and the Church." What precisely does Paul have in mind when he uses the word *mystery*? Does he refer to the marriage relation between man and woman (here expressly taken as physical), or does he use the word to signify the relationship between Christ and the Church alone, or is he recalling the legend of paradise (to which he has alluded in the previous verse), that Eve was fashioned from Adam's rib as prototype and parable of the Church's formation from Christ? We can leave this question open, because whatever the precise reference of the word *mystery*, it is evident that the passage as a whole refers to the entire complex, namely: conjugal relationships—that is, sexual relationships ordered to a higher purpose— cannot exist outside the encompassing radiance of Christ's relationship to his Church, for which relationship the origin of Eve from Adam is and will always remain an eloquent parable. It is the mystery of Christ, though, that bestows upon marriage, as on all lesser relationships, its character of mystery.

We ought not to forget here that for Paul marriage is by no means the only way of being a follower of the Christ-mystery. In the First Letter to the Corinthians he points to the way of virginity and gives it preference when it means "being concerned about the Lord's affairs and seeking to please the Lord" (7:32). It is the way of Paul himself, and "I should like all men to be as I am. . . . To the unmarried and to the widows I say that they do well if they remain as I am" (7:7–8). In saying this, Paul is only repeating what Christ himself had lived and praised as a special charism. When lived in the spirit of Christ, the way of virginity is clearly a more direct imitation of Christ's relationship to the Church and of his perfect fruitfulness. And yet the Redeemer of the world is also the one who brings the order of creation to perfection, and he opens up marriage, grounded as it is in the order of creation, so that it becomes a way to follow him in a very specific manner.

The first sentence of our text brings us to the core of the statement: "Submit to one another in the fear of Christ." This fear of Christ certainly has nothing to do with a sense of terror that would alienate us from Christ. The *fear* Paul has in mind is the Old Testament sense of awe before the divine majesty of our Creator, Redeemer and Judge. "The fear of God is the beginning of wisdom" (Wis 1:7). So also the fear of Christ is the beginning of all Christian married life, a life that cannot be regulated by norms and laws of one's own invention, but only by the norm that is Christ himself and his manner of life.

It is wholly impossible for the injunction "Submit to one another" to apply only to the wives and not also to their husbands, since the same admonition is addressed even more frequently to Christians in general. We have already quoted the passage from Philippians, and in Galatians Paul repeats Christ's commandment: "Out of [Christian] love, place yourselves at one another's service" (5:13). Here the word is *douleuein*, which actually means "to perform the offices of a slave". And the First Letter of Peter demands: "In your dealings with one another, all of you should clothe yourselves in humility"—and this was said just after the rule had been given that the younger should submit to the older (5:5). The elders—the leaders—are to be no less humble than the young men; otherwise, how could they represent the Lord of the Church, who, though our "Lord and Master", lived among us "as a servant" (Jn 12:13ff.)? Now we can go on with our text.

> Submit to one another in the fear of Christ. Wives should be submissive to their husbands as if to the Lord, because the husband is head of the wife just as Christ is head of his body the Church, as well as its savior. As the Church submits to Christ, so wives should submit to their husbands in everything (Eph 5:21–24).

For the time being let us leave aside the troublesome statement that the husband is the head of his wife. Later on we shall have to ask to what extent this statement is historically conditioned, to what extent not. What concerns us now is a statement which is certainly *not* historically conditioned, namely, that Christ is the head of the Church, and indeed her head because he is her Redeemer—*soter*. This means that all members of the Church, men and women, have every reason to submit to Christ. The fact that Christ is here described as *Redeemer of his body*, and not Redeemer of his Bride or of his Spouse, may cause surprise; but the words we expect follow soon. The well-known image of Christ as *head and body* is given first so that it will be evident that the Church owes her entire being to Christ. The Church has first been brought forth from his fullness, and then, in a second movement, she turns to him, herself a living vessel for his fruitfulness. With regard to this, her ultimate meaning, the Church is feminine. She is receptive and nurturing; she gives birth to what she, as Christ's fruitfulness, has received from him. Israel was often enough described as *bride* and *spouse* of her God, and the Church continues and intensifies Israel's relationship with Yahweh, being always feminine in reference to her God. Christians from the first centuries to the Middle Ages always thought of the Church as a woman and so represented her: *Mater Ecclesia,*

Sponsa Christi—and this despite the fact of the hierarchy being composed solely of men. These men are the agents of Christ the Bridegroom within the Church's all-embracing femininity. Her femininity was even more strongly emphasized in the Church of the Fathers and of the Middle Ages by the fact that the Church was seen as united with the Virgin Mother Mary and indeed was often made almost identical with her. This identity flows from two sources. First, Mary, the virginal Mother, was appointed by Christ on the Cross to be the Mother of all Christians and in this sense to be his Bride. Second, through the sacraments, particularly baptism and the Eucharist, the Church herself bears all Christians as Christ's members in her womb and nurtures them, thus becoming the mystical Mother of Christ.

Let us go a step further now and focus on the statement that follows: that Christ gave himself up (on the Cross) for his Church in order to make her a "spotless, holy and immaculate" Bride and so to present her to himself (5:27). And if we search out where it is that the Church fully meets this description, we again encounter the Woman who is the Immaculate One par excellence. We will also realize that, even as Mother of the Lord, Mary acquired her quality as *Immaculata* from her Son, and indeed from his Cross. As Mother, Mary

clearly possesses and exercises authority over her
Child; in Luke we read explicitly that "he sub-
mitted to them" (*hypotassomenos autois*: 2:51). But
it is only by virtue of her Son's Cross that Mary,
redeemed by the Cross before the event, possesses
the right and the capacity to bring up and shelter
the Son of God.

Once we have truly seen and understood the
role of Mary, we may turn to the problem presented to us by Paul's words: "Wives should be
submissive to their husbands . . . because the husband is the head of his wife" (5:22–23). One might
begin by objecting that this statement is obviously
historically conditioned, since Paul appears to demand submission only from those members of
society who are, in fact, in an inferior position:
women must submit to men, children to their
fathers, slaves to their masters (Eph 6:1–5; Col
3:18, 20, 22). In so doing, he simply accepts the
ancient social order as given; even, for example,
when it assigns to fathers (and not to mothers)
the responsibility of rearing their children. Then
too, the ancient view of procreation may form
a considerable part of the background of Paul's
thought: the view, that is, that in procreation only
the man plays an active, effective role, while the
woman is merely passive and receptive, and that
the nature of woman may be defined by a de-
ficiency which makes her a *mas occasionatum*, a

male *manqué*. (This view persisted even into High and Late Scholasticism.)

Now, this idea of the inferiority of women in the social order was demolished and left behind long ago, precisely as a result of Christianity, which stresses the equal dignity of women. And the ancient theory of procreation has been thoroughly refuted by the insights of modern biology, which has realized that in the conception of a child the woman's organism is just as active as the man's. Indeed, by reason of the long pregnancy, birth, the stages of feeding, and subsequent child care on the mother's part, we could say that the woman exhibits an activity which is significantly superior to the man's.

And there is more. I can only speak here as one interested in science but with no special authority, but what I speak of is a pivotal finding of modern genetic research. Competent biologists have expressed the view that the basic embryonic structure of all living beings, including man, is primarily feminine, and the subsequent differentiation of the male arises from a tendency toward extreme formations, while the development of the female shows a persistence in the original balance.[1] If this is correct—and it certainly corresponds to an instinctive feeling that the womb of the *Natura*

[1] Cf. Adolf Portmann, "Die biologischen Grundfragen der Typenlehre", in *Eranos* 1974 (Leiden: Brill, 1977), 449–73.

naturans is feminine—then we would have to reverse the scholastic definition of woman as a *mas occasionatum* and define the male, rather, as a *femina occasionata*, a woman *manquée*. However it may be, it is certain that the active power of the female organism as it forms the child in the womb, gives it birth and nourishes it will (precisely if we contemplate it in the light of contemporary biology) make us see all created Being as essentially feminine when compared to the Creator God. From the beginning, matter requires the action of God: it is he who must bestow upon it the power to produce out of itself all the increasingly complex forms of life. And from this perspective we could say that the Church's relationship to Christ is the ultimate realization of the creature's relationship to God, since God has placed the creature in existence outside himself and endowed it with the inner ability to nurture the seed it has received and, in turn, to send the seed out into its own life.

From all this we can now draw two conclusions that may answer the question whether the concept of man and woman displayed in our text is not perhaps historically conditioned and therefore dispensable.

The first thing that is said in our text is that the relationship between man and woman in marriage is an image of the relationship between Christ and the Church and must pattern itself after the norm of that relationship. The decisive norm for the man–woman relationship is thus a *theological norm*, not a norm patterned on the social customs of a particular time. This point is very clearly impressed on us by the verse that follows: "Husbands, love your wives, as Christ loved the Church. He gave himself up for her" (5:25). And again we read, "In any case, each one should love his wife as he loves himself" (5:33, cf. 28)—that is, as his own body—in the manner, therefore, in which Christ has loved his own body, the Church. This theological norm for the relationship between the sexes provides us with a sound guiding principle in applying the message of Paul to the problems of *Humanae Vitae*.

But before going on, we must make a second point that emerges from a comparison of the relationship between the sexes with the far superior archetype of the Christ–Church relationship. Christ does something that a husband can in no way do: Christ brings forth the Church from himself as his own fullness, as his body, and, finally, as his Bride. By his self-surrender, he confers upon the Church the form and structure he desires, the life of the Holy Spirit that is a counterpart to his own life. The husband, on the other hand, encounters his wife as a separate person, with her own freedom and her own act of surrender to him—a freedom and a surrender that he does not create. The husband also realizes that, as we have seen, his wife possesses a feminine fruitfulness that is her own and stems even less from him.

Nevertheless, it does not seem to me that this simply invalidates the statement about the husband being the head of his wife. Prescinding from any and every social system (patriarchal or matriarchal) and from all theories of procreation (ancient, scholastic or modern), it always remains true that in sexual intercourse it is the man who is the initiator, the leader, the shaper, while the woman's love—even if it is not passive, but just as active in its own way—is still essentially receptive. We could almost say (very naively) that, through the man, the woman is somehow awakened to herself, to the fullness of her feminine self-awareness. This initiative on the man's part is something primary that sets in motion the whole process of feminine fruitfulness. Such an order of things holds true even if we may smile at the incidental, marginal and transitory character of the male's function in procreation, a function that certainly cannot be compared with Christ's extraordinary act of self-surrender.

But it still remains true that the absolute beginning lies in the progenitor—in the father—while the feminine principle, even as *Magna Mater* or as *Mother Nature*, can never be simply conceived as the beginning. In the Christian view of God, the begetting Father stands at the very source and origin of all things. This Father, to be sure, is incomparably superior to all earthly fatherhood. As a divine Person, God the Father is eternally identical with his act of procreation, and of all creation only One is able to present to us a valid image of the Father: Jesus Christ, who creates the Church from the totality of his divine and human substance, which he surrenders on the Cross. The begetting power of Jesus Christ, which is what creates the Church, is his Eucharist, and over and beyond all times and places it is this Eucharist that makes the Church forever present. This power of Christ is the perfect image of the eternal Father precisely because neither Christ nor the Father holds anything back for himself or places any reservations on his own self-surrender; they have no fear of losing themselves through this perfect outpouring and lavishing of themselves. Unlike the man in the act of intercourse, Christ does not give away just a little of his substance. No, Christ gives away his entire substance, just as the eternal Father, in begetting the Son, makes over to the Son his entire divine substance, and then again both of them give this substance over to the Holy Spirit, without division, in an act of communal love.

In the act of procreation, the man represents

only a distant analogy to this trinitarian and christological event. But it is an analogy nonetheless;
and this analogy allows us to acknowledge, even
today, the truth contained in the statement that the
husband is the head of his wife. The husband,
however, must be aware that his action stands
under a norm, under a head, just as Christ, in his
self-surrender to the Church, is ever mindful that
in his action in the world he is carrying out his
mission: to represent the goodness of the Father
who gives of himself eternally. So Paul says in the
First Letter to the Corinthians: "You should know
that Christ is the head of every man, and the man
is the head of the woman, and God the head of
Christ" (11:3). And if the word *head* appears awkward here, we could instead say: that superior
reality which at the same time bestows and releases
power, but always along with it a norm according
to which that power is to be exercised.

From all this we have gained one general insight:
for the Christian husband and for the Christian
wife, the norm of their sexual relationship is a
theological one, namely, the relationship between
Christ and the Church. We could say that this
holds true for all *non*-Christians as well, only
they know nothing of this norm and therefore
cannot consciously pattern themselves after it. It
must suffice here to speak of this norm insofar

as it concerns Christians. We cannot examine here the ways in which conscious conformity to this norm, conscious participation in Christ's activity, makes Christian marriage a sacrament. And our text from Paul does not deal with this question, although it does speak of the great mystery (*sacramentum*). But the word *sacramentum* here refers to the whole structure; it refers to the relationship between Christ and the Church and to this relationship as the all-embracing sphere within which the marriage relationship between husband and wife has its existence.

Before we conclude by reflecting explicitly on *Humanae Vitae*, we must insert an additional observation that seems important to our text. We have previously spoken of the ephemeral nature of the man's contribution in setting in motion the great process of feminine fruitfulness. And yet, in the sexual act, the man does give from what is his, and if he is to stand under the norm of Christ, he *ought* not only give *something* of what is his, but must rather surrender *his very self*, just as the eternal Father surrenders his very self and everything that is his in order to beget the Son. If the husband does this, he will come all the closer to Christ, who by his self-surrender fashions his own Mystical Body.

This is why our text also says: "Husbands should

love their wives as they do their own bodies", for no one hates his own body, but rather "nourishes it and takes care of it as Christ cares for the Church." And then we are referred to the great passage in Genesis where we read that: "For this reason a man shall leave his father and mother and shall cling to his wife, and the two shall be made into one" (Eph 5:28b–31). For Christ this means that on the Cross and in the Eucharist he gives of his Flesh and his Blood so unreservedly that in what results from this self-surrender—that is, in the Church as a separate being outside himself—Christ finds himself again. This rediscovery of himself in the Church would not be possible if Christ had only half given himself and half kept himself back. If we reflect from this perspective on the husband's part in the sexual act, we will see that he can do justice to the commandment to love his wife as his own body *only* if he hands himself over to her unconditionally, so that from now on he can recognize in her all that he has surrendered —that is, his entire self.

We can now sense the magnitude of what is demanded. What man can do justice to it? Truly, a supernatural measure of selflessness is required in order to bring a man to such love as this, possessive as he is by nature and rendered selfish in his sexuality by sin. Man *needs* woman in order to release and satisfy himself, even though he may also feel the impulse of love, strong or weak, genuine or imaginary. And very often he loves the woman as his own body, which he nourishes and looks after, in an egotistical sense, a sense that is the exact opposite of what our text means. The Middle Ages, with its realistic bent of mind, spoke of the *remedium concupiscentiae* ("remedy for lust"), in stern contrast to our modern sexual theories, which are mostly unrealistic and idyllic, and trivialize sexuality. Paul is himself a realist when in the First Letter to the Corinthians he recommends: "Those who do not have the strength to abstain ought to marry, for it is better to marry than to burn [with desire]" (7:9).

In love, as in fidelity, the woman has an easier time of it. As we have said, she is creatureliness itself with regard to God, and with regard to Christ she is the very image of the Church. The woman is not called upon to represent anything that she herself is not, while the man has to represent the very source of life, which he can never *be*.

We now take up the question of *Humanae Vitae* by affirming that the highest of all relationships, that between Christ and the Church, is by its nature a fruitful one. The notion of fruitfulness is basic in the New Testament: just think of the parables of growth, the parable of the barren tree that must be cut down, and particularly the parable of the vine and the branches. The Church herself embodies the fruitfulness of Christ, and together with him she is again to bear fruit—"fruits of the Spirit" (Gal 5:22), "fruits of the light" (Eph 5:9), "fruits of justice" (Phil 1:11, James 3:18). It goes without saying that the concept of fruitfulness brings us into a sphere that affects every Christian, without distinction between the married and those who have consecrated their virginity to God. We have only to think of Mary, whose physical fruitfulness is itself the fruit of her faith and her virginity. And yet it is from the fruitfulness of Christ and the Church that the model for the married state may be drawn. For the source of this fruitfulness lies in the fact that no limits whatsoever are imposed on self-surrender, either on Christ's part or on that of the Church. Christ's eucharistic self-surrender on the Cross is absolutely unreserved: reckless, we might say. He abandons himself to the abyss of sin; he gives himself to those who are unworthy of him, a gift symbolized by the morsel he hands to Judas. And in Mary, at least, there is a loving readiness to receive, equally unreserved. Her assent means that she can be led in any direction, even into places and situations that she neither knows nor suspects. It is precisely this attitude that is the source of all Christian fruitfulness, not the performance of any calculated and well-planned "good works" whatever.

We find a striking comparison of these two attitudes in the story of the supper at Bethany. On one hand we have Mary's anointing of Jesus, an expression of her boundless surrender to him. And Jesus takes up her surrender and makes it part of the divine plan of salvation, an anointing for his Passion. Mary takes on the role of the loving Church, ministering to Jesus in acceptance of his eucharistic self-surrender—*personam Ecclesia gerens*, as the Fathers say. On the other hand, we have Judas: "What is the good of this waste? Why wasn't the oil sold, and the money given to the poor? It was worth more than three hundred denarii." Sound thinking, one might say, but the evangelist unmasks its secret egotism.

Let us turn back now to human marriage. The union of husband and wife means more than merely physical fruitfulness, the begetting of children; it means spiritual fruitfulness as well, total surrender to each other. Now, the conjunction in man of the physical and the spiritual involves an inherent ambiguity, for these two aspects of his life are altogether inseparable. Man is at once body and spirit. He is a member of an animal species in which procreation, birth and death are interdependent; and at the same time he is person and spirit, superior to all other species. Because of this conjunction of animal and spiritual he cannot remain a person without remaining a member of his species. Therefore, he cannot divert a species-oriented function from its inherent purpose solely in order to satisfy his own personal desires. Or rather, he *can* do so, but not without schizophrenically splitting his own inner organic unity. For when he acts in this way, he sets his own personal limits on a function of the human species, a function with its own inner finality. Ostensibly, he limits his fertility in this manner so that he can give fuller emphasis to the limitless, personal side of his being. But in so doing he obviously introduces an element of calculation and limitation into an act that is meant to be the symbolic expression of an unconditional love between man and woman.

All of us are aware of the social problems to which the indissoluble duality of man's sexual nature can lead, both at the family level and at the wider level of state and society as a whole. It should not surprise us, then, that as their problems grow more severe, men are easily persuaded to adopt the lesser of two evils: that is, to introduce calculation into an act which in its perfection is beyond all calculation. As the encyclical states, one can find all sorts of excuses for such behavior. People take as their ultimate argument the fact that the distinctive part of man's nature is his ability to master the physical and biological world, and shape it to his own needs and purposes.

When men no longer see themselves bound by the norm of that love which exists between Christ and the Church, one can hardly convince them that their arrogation of full power to regulate the procreative function puts all truly personal love between man and woman in serious jeopardy. And the task is all the more difficult because in the present post-Christian era most men have already lost all vision of the unique and eternal dignity of the person. This loss of vision is equally evident in both halves of the world—in that half where the individual is seen as a mere function of economic laws, and in the other half, too, where the word *freedom* is still written large, but where the fundamental sciences of life are psychology and sociology.

The Christian couple today lives in a society beset with dangers and uncertainties unprecedented in human history, and they will have no easy life if they desire to make the absolute love of Christ and his Church the rule of their lives. But this love itself will guide the couple along a path they can follow.

The wellspring of the whole Christian life is certainly the spirit of faith, hope and love, a will to engage in a total, not a partial, imitation of Christ, an enduring endeavor to remove the barriers against Christ that we are always putting up, sinners and self-worshippers that we are. And when a man and a woman live this sort of life, keeping before their eyes Christ's eucharistic love and Mary's assent, they will inevitably find themselves restrained from debasing their acts of married love, acts that are intended by their very nature to express an unlimited and self-giving love.

But does not society itself impose such limitations on married love with irresistible force? Does society not exert such moral pressure on married people that they cannot follow the norms of Christ unreservedly? The encyclical answers these questions by saying that, before society began to make such demands, nature itself had come to man's aid by establishing a periodic rhythm in the days of a woman's physical fertility. (I emphasize the word *physical*, for her spiritual fertility, which is supernatural and flows from grace, has no periods.) And there is all the difference in the world between using one's awareness of the periods of infertility and arrogating to oneself the right to impose radical restrictions on fertility by the use of artificial contraception.

Many see little difference here. And perhaps

226

there is little difference, so long as man views himself as an entity that invents itself and regulates itself: *homo technicus*. Were this view of man the truth, no limits at all could be set on his manipulation of his own nature.

But the difference is great to the eyes of any man or woman who thinks as a Christian. For in using the infertile days they are not setting bounds to their love. Otherwise, one would have to say that intercourse in the full Christian sense is impossible after a woman's menopause. Married persons who think as Christians set no barriers between the two objects of marriage: procreation and the expression of mutual love. They let the two stand together, the physical side, with its own proper laws, and the personal side. One's awareness of the opportunities provided by nature does not mean that one is imposing calculation on the inner spirit of love.

Let us end with this observation. For sexuality as Christians understand it—sexuality that takes as its norm the relationship between Christ and his Church—Christ's words hold true: "Let him grasp it who can." But Christ is saying something more here than that very few men and women will actually grasp his doctrine. He is issuing us a challenge to serious endeavor, the same challenge, essentially, that rings through the whole of the

227

Gospel: take up your cross every day, sell all you possess, and do not cheat as did Ananias and Sapphira. Why should the sexual area alone offer no challenge to the Christian? Sexuality, even as *eros*, is to be an expression of *agape*, and *agape* always involves an element of renunciation. And only by renunciation can the limits that we set on our own self-surrender be transcended.

I think that only Christians can understand the challenge posed by *Humanae Vitae*, and even Christians only to the degree that they strive to follow Christ as married persons, and keep his example before their eyes with ever-increasing devotion. For all of them—men and women—are, after all, sons and daughters of the Church, who owes her existence to Christ and who raises her eyes to him with reverence and awe, his loving Bride (Eph 5:33).

OBEDIENCE IN THE LIGHT OF THE GOSPEL

This title immediately unfolds into several pairs in tension. First of all, there is the obedience of Jesus, which is basic to everything, and the obedience of the disciples to Jesus. The former would seem to be qualitatively different than the latter, and yet they belong together.

Then, within the Church proceeding from the disciples, there is an element of each Christian's direct obedience to God in Jesus Christ; this obedience, however, is always mediated by the Church, and more specifically by the hierarchy.

Finally, in this Church there is on the one hand the tension just mentioned, which affects all Christians, and in addition a charismatic obedience, sanctioned by the Church, in the way of life according to the evangelical counsels. The second and third tensions, in order to be really Christian, are necessarily founded in the first: in the correlation of Christ's unique obedience to his call to discipleship.

How are all these tensions related? In order to attain clarity, we must start with Christ's prototypical obedience. But is it really prototypical for the Church? Is it not much easier and more unproblematic to obey God directly, as he does, than to obey human beings as well, who with authority mediate something of God's will to the Christian in the Church in general and in the religious life in particular?

1. The Obedience of Jesus
and the Obedience of the Disciples

a. The Obedience of Jesus

Jesus has a gigantic mission: to reconcile the world to God. This absolutely universal mission implies that Jesus must be more than a mere human being in order to be capable of carrying out such a task. But since he is true man, he must have a humanly surveyable mission, namely, to lead the chosen people back to its proper role: that of being legitimate partner in the covenant with God and thus becoming in the midst of the world the mountain of salvation to which the peoples will come in pilgrimage. Thus, in the specificity of his human mission, its universality is indirectly contained.

But Jesus' mission is akin to that of the prophets. Isaiah is sent originally to Israel with God's salvific word and is told at the same time that his mission will fail: similarly with Jeremiah and Ezechiel. Like these prophets, Jesus will fail in his life mission. But to life belongs death, the "hour"—of darkness as well as of the Father—in which he will no longer accomplish anything in a human way; but in a divinely human way (beyond human powers) he will bear and bear away, as God's scapegoat, all the world's resistance and sin, inwardly victorious in outward failure, because his will to do the Father's will above and beyond human capability lets itself be laden with the burden of it all. The whole, in all its anonymity, the *hamartia* [sin], which nevertheless includes each individual by name, he really takes upon himself; how, we shall never know. It is a mystery. But the key expression for this work of the triune God's love is consenting passivity, obedience. That is what the Apostles' Creed is about.

Let us cast a few sidelights on the interpretation with which the New Testament reverently encompasses this mystery. The first thing we encounter, in the light of the Resurrection, is insight into the *"pro nobis"* (1 Cor 15:3f.), and this "according to the Scriptures" (ibid.), since Jesus embodies the sin-bearing Servant of God already mentioned in the first apostolic sermons. The formula "for us" is certainly pre-Pauline, and so is the central interpretation in the hymn contained in Philippians: self-emptying of the form of God in order to become obedient unto death. Here and in other hymns, and soon afterwards in Paul, Jesus' act of reconciliation appears as the victory over the powers and dominions inimical to God.

Paul builds his cathedral on this preexisting

foundation. The *"pro nobis"* is its innermost sanctum. But the self-surrender of Christ, who did not "live to please himself" but took upon himself the shame of others (Rom 15:3f.), is ultimately the Father's surrender of the Son for us (Rom 8:32), in which God's entire salvific plan from Abraham and Moses onwards is fulfilled at the same time: Jesus was, after all, "born of woman" (and therefore grew up in human obedience), "subject to the law" (Gal 4:4), which he on the one hand superabundantly fulfilled (Mt 5:17) and by which on the other hand he was slain (Gal 3:13) because it did not want to let itself be restored to its essential truth, the covenant with the living God. In the hour of absolute obedience, Jesus fulfilled not only the inner salvation history of Israel but also his eschatological mission of calling all peoples (Is 49:6). It is precisely on the Cross, in the surrendered, sacrificed body of Jesus, that the dividing wall is demolished (Eph 2:14).

The Letter to the Hebrews makes explicit the paradox latent in Paul: that Jesus' commission is as timeless as his decision to become man—freely entering the world, he wants to do God's will (Heb 10:5ff.)—and that as man he nevertheless had to "learn" this difficult obedience experientially ("with tears": Heb 5:7f.).

Among the Synoptics, Luke most strongly underscores Jesus' human obedience even as a child and youth, as well as his parents' obedience to the law at the Purification in the Temple ("in keeping with the law of the Lord"; "in keeping with the law of Moses"), at which the Holy Spirit of freedom breathes. Later the twelve-year-old Jesus stresses obedience to the heavenly Father as basis and aim of his existence. Matthew likewise portrays Jesus fulfilling the law even to the last jot, thereby transcending all the ancient justice. The Jesus of the Synoptics lives and continually proclaims the paradox of his being Lord and Master yet the servant of all, even to surrendering his life—eucharistically—as ransom "for the many". At least from the time of Caesarea Philippi onward, he lives steadfastly intent on the "hour", the baptism that he is awaiting—and "how constrained I am until it is accomplished" (Lk 12:50). The "must" hanging over his head is the Father's will, which is to be done on earth as in heaven, that God's kingdom may come; and it comes through him, through the tremendous event of the "hour".

John declares that Jesus is quite simply the one who is sent, who does not do his own will, seek his own honor or proclaim his own teaching, but the will, honor and teaching of the Father. There is no passivity in this. If he is the one whom the

233

Father gives up out of love for the world, he is at the same time the Shepherd who freely gives up his life for his sheep, his friends. Active and passive elements coincide in his submission to the Father's will: in *letting* himself be given up, he *gives* himself, and vice versa. Here, even in the Synoptics, the mystery of the Holy Spirit comes to the fore. In the Incarnation, at the baptism, in the temptation, in the public life, it is the Holy Spirit who actively impels; Jesus is the one impelled by him, not from without, heteronomously, but from above as well as from within. He is *the* pneumatic one, possessing the Spirit without measure. But the Spirit hovers at the same time *over* him as the objective mediator of the Father's will, like a rule that in suffering can become so strict that it eclipses the loving Father's countenance. This position of the Spirit answers the question we raised at the beginning: it is not easier—rather, it is incomparably harder—to obey God's demands, which present the Spirit as their rule and concern the reconciliation of the whole world, than it is to obey a human being in the Church who indicates reasonable commands of God.

The Son's unique obedience is all-embracing. Before the foundation of the world, we have been chosen in him and reconciled in his blood (Eph 1).

Alpha and Omega, he is the Lamb slain from the beginning of the world.

Let us summarize his obedience in three paradoxes:

1. As *God*-Man, he is the identity of love and obedience, insofar as his *missio* is the appearance in this world of his *processio* in God: the revelation of the Father. From all eternity, in the divine spontaneity of the consubstantial Son, he is in accord with the Father in the Holy Spirit and offers himself for the completion of the work of creation. He loves mankind and offers himself for each individual, because and as the Father loves all and gives the Son for the sake of those he loves. Thus, in him there is no tension between love for the Father and love for mankind. And the authority by which he represents the Father is one with his humility, with which he manifests the Father.

2. As *God-Man* he is the exact translation and reproduction of the divinity in human speech and form—as exact as the copy Moses makes of the heavenly sanctuary in the covenant tent, as exact as the symbolic actions the prophets carry out in obedience—but this in the full human spontaneity and creativity evident in all his actions. He is completely beyond the tension between literal and pneumatic obedience.

3. As God-*Man* he makes his obedience incar-

nate in that of the ordinary human life that he
assumes by transcending it to perfection. He obeys
his family (and all the laws of human communication for thirty years), but as a youth of twelve
transcends this obedience for the sake of obedience
to the Father. He obeys the state and religion,
giving Caesar his due and paying the temple tax,
but at the same time he stresses the freedom
of sons.

b. The Obedience of the disciples

We may not consider the obedience of the disciples
only in its imperfect phase during Jesus' earthly
life; we must also consider it in its full practicability
by means of the Eucharist and the outpouring of
the Spirit.

Jesus made his divine-human obedience incarnate in his obedience on the purely human level:
that is to say, on the one hand, into the community
of free spirit-subjects, each of whom has to recognize the rights of the other in order to make life
together possible; on the other hand, within a
community possessing a familial authority and a
civil authority protecting and representing the
rights of the individual and the welfare of all. But
Jesus, as the new Adam, transformed from within
this structure of community and authority in the

old adamic humanity by assuming in his Passion the place of each sinful subject, by laying a new elemental foundation of community in his Eucharist and in his sending of the Spirit and at the same time embodying in this new community his authority, which points to the Father. Thus three steps are required of Jesus' disciples in following him.

1. They must leave everything that binds them to the old adamic community, in order to begin anew in Jesus' loving obedience: together with him, born of God, receiving the kingdom like a child, sent by Jesus as he is sent by the Father. This new beginning and this mission are so little heteronomous and alienating that in them we arrive for the first time at our qualitatively unique personality; we con-form ourselves to God's idea of us from all eternity, thus being converted from slaves to free children (cf. Eph 1:3ff.). In his ultimate reality, Simon son of John is Peter the Rock. Rebirth and mission grant a share in the (eternal) uniqueness of the only begotten Son's relationship to the Father. To carry out one's mission, placing oneself entirely at its disposal, means to fulfill oneself and thus to attain to personal freedom and self-fulfillment: childhood and maturity are one.

2. The newly motivated persons are placed in a

relationship to one another based on Christ. It is no longer a matter of merely recognizing the rights of other people; rather, according to Jesus' example, it is a question of vital service to one's neighbor. The "greater", more Christian person is the person who serves more deeply; like Jesus, who serves at the eucharistic table and washes the feet of his enemy, Judas. Mutual obedience proceeds from obedience to God in leaving everything. "The servant is not greater than his master. If I, your Lord and master, have washed your feet, you too must wash one another's feet" (Jn 13:16, 15). Similarly, Paul says: "Bear one another's burdens, and thus you will fulfill Christ's law" (Gal 6:2). "Have the same attitude among yourselves as Christ Jesus had. Let each one think better of the others than of himself, each looking out not for his own interests only, but also for those of the others" (Phil 2:5, 3f.). "Submit to one another in the fear of Christ" (Eph 5:21). This ethical command rests on the foundation of the ontic Christian community, founded by means of the Eucharist and the outpouring of the Spirit: his Church, which as locus and vessel of Christ's self-effusive fullness is anterior to the individual member and requires each one's Christlike self-giving to the other members.

3. In the Christian community, the principle of authority inherent in every adamic community—

family or state—is recast into an authority expressly originating with Jesus, by which he shares his own unique authority. First of all this authority is general, in that each one called to be a disciple receives authority to proclaim Christ's message ("anyone who hears you hears me"), to cast out the unclean spirit, and to bind and to loose; and these powers will live on primarily in the Church's bishops. Second, he grants Peter a place of primacy by which Peter, in his own person and in his successors, is able to do on a universal scale what the others can do in their own commissioned sphere. To see the extent of this, we need only look at Paul, who, above all in the Second Letter to the Corinthians, anticipating the Church's entire history, runs through the list of all the tensions and problems and all the profound, fruitful mysteries of this ecclesial obedience.

This leads us to the second section, to the tension of inner-ecclesial obedience between immediate obedience to God, immediate obedience to neighbor and the mediation of Church authority.

2. The Obedience of the Christian in the Church of Christ

The Holy Spirit, placed in the heart of the Christian, immediately makes him a brother of Christ and thus a son of the Father. And in the Spirit the Christian receives the "anointing" that leads him into the whole, indivisible truth (Jn 16:13), "teaches" him "about everything" (1 Jn 2:27) and also gives him—directly from God (Rom 12:3) and from Christ—a personalizing charism.

Yet this charism (Eph 4:11) is essentially service to the community (1 Cor 12:7). It can develop only in the community, therefore, in love lived out (1 Cor 12): together with all the saints (Eph 3:18), who can make the enmeshed "joints" of the "body of Christ", which is being built up, function (Eph 4:16f.) by means of mutual assistance, instruction and exhortation. This second, social aspect itself shows that, in order to identify with his mission, the individual cannot look only at an individual ideal of himself in God. Rather, together with the others, he has to view the communal ideal of an *ecclesia immaculata* and thus *infallibilis* (Eph 5:27). This ideal cannot be pure ideality but must possess reality, since Christ, as a man and the head of the ecclesial community, is obliged to the community in certain respects. The pure disponibility of the Virgin Mother is the space-affording medium within which every charismatic service can develop as a service of love and to which the serving Christian must attend, if he is to live out his mission in a sufficiently open,

240

catholic manner instead of narrowly and egotistically. This is because the Christian sinner as an individual will time and again succumb to the illusion that he is doing God's will when in reality he is only following his own inclinations; consequently, the community of Christian sinners will do the same.

Hence the indispensability of a mediating authority becomes evident, to lead both the individual and the community to the pure, complete development of their mission. The authority— and this is fundamentally important—rests on the baptized Christian's fundamental Yes to the entire Word of God (and thus does not represent coercion from without); but where the sinful, imperfect Christian hesitates or refuses, it will hold up to him the consequences of his own assent, specify them for him and help him to carry them out.

The individual and the community need not furnish this authority for themselves; it has been instituted by Christ as the ecclesial office, which is indispensable to love, and which has its own essential and intrinsic dialectic.

For, on the one hand, the purpose of the office— or, more precisely, the office holder—is to point with authority to the ideal and to the rule that is above everyone, namely, to the concrete and pneumatic Christ as he shows himself in Scripture to be authentic and accessible for all the faithful. It is not enough, however, merely to point; every Christian can do the same. The ecclesial office must also be able authoritatively to actualize, re-present, what it points to; for this purpose Christ has conferred on it the *exousia*, authority (to teach, to make present sacramentally, to govern legitimately). These two functions of the office holder are inseparable: as the one who points out, he is, together with all the other members, obviously subject to the norm. In Peter's denial of his Lord we are strikingly reminded of this. But as representative of the norm, he more than all the others has the duty to make his life coincide as closely as possible with his official mission. He has to represent not only formal authority but also a humanly credible authority, not by identifying himself with Christ or with the gospel—the pope is not the successor or representative of Christ, but of Peter—but by pointing to Christ in an existentially convincing manner. In so doing, he surmounts in the Christian sphere what is generally valid on the human level: for example, that a judge has to interpret the law governing the community in an authoritative and existentially trustworthy way in order to make it possible in the first place for the community to be authentically human.

From this constellation, there follow decisive consequences both for those obeying and for those commanding.

a. In virtue of the Spirit's anointing, it is possible for *one who obeys* to compare ecclesial authority's allusion to the evangelical norm with the norm itself, and possibly to ascertain such a divergence between them that his ecclesial conscience compels him to prefer the gospel norm that seems judicious to him rather than the concrete directive of the authorities. This would certainly be the case if the command prescribed something culpably deviating from the norm. It is, however, not the case when authority prescribes something less good than what I conceive on my own. This is so, first of all, because I do not obey as an isolated individual but "together with all the saints"; thus, my conscience must always take into account its ecclesial dimension. Further, obedience to an authority instituted by the Church and ultimately by Christ is a value that can weigh more than insistence on one's own insight, however superior it may be. After all, Christ too, at least in the Passion, rendered an injudicious obedience by which, at the moment of being overtaxed, he atoned for Adam's disobedience and priggishness.

A fragile balance exists between obedience to a norm deemed judicious by the believing conscience (an obedience that also allows an open contestation and fraternal correction of the office holder), the Christian's appeal to the *sensus fidelium* of the universal Church, and concrete authority instituted by Christ (no distinction between *sedes* and *sedens*!). This balance can be soundly maintained only by a person with living faith; and in today's Church, it absolutely must be maintained. The *sensus fidelium*, the collective conscience within a vital ecclesial tradition, can in this respect constitute a kind of safe middle between overbearing self-allocation of the absolute evangelical norm and a defeatist, blind obedience; but the opinion that one really possesses this *sensus fidelium* can likewise be subject to all sorts of illusions, traditional or progressive.

Nor may we forget here that there are various degrees and holders of authority in the Church. It is quite possible that at certain times direct obedience to a bishop or a group of bishops can become problematic and perhaps impossible—for instance, if a bishops' conference should let itself be terrorized by the advisory councils or *bureaux permanents* that it has appointed—while one can very well adhere to the clear orthodoxy and the convincing *martyrion* of a pope. At other times in the Church's history, the opposite has also occurred.

All this shows that the catchwords "pyramidal" or "spherical" (paternalistic or democratic) obedience are not genuine alternatives. Although those entrusted with an office are absolutely *in* the ecclesial community, still the office itself does not emanate *from* the community but is instituted in the Church from above. Later, when we compare ecclesial and religious obedience, this will be the criterion for distinguishing them. This "from above" is christological grace that enables Christians, both as individuals and as a community, to imitate Christ's obedience to the Father, granted by God and mediated by the Holy Spirit objectified as rule.

b. The official mission of the *one who commands* entails the imperative of making his life a witness (*martyrion*) to what he represents. Paul does this in grand style when he presents himself as the exemplary *typos* of the Church because his life portrays Christ's life and suffering and, what is more, contains them sacramentally. On the other hand, he knows precisely where to draw the line. He who is "crucified with Christ" (Gal 2:19) can indignantly ask: "Was Paul by any chance crucified for you, or were you baptized in Paul's name?" (1 Cor 1:13). He offers no foothold to Donatists; his whole existence is pure reference to the norm that rules and judges him as well as everyone else (1 Cor 4:4).

Peter's case is the exact reverse. With his appointment to office, his life (as denier) and the demands of his office (to love, not just in any way,

245

but "more than these") split intolerably asunder. Who will ever want or be able to recognize as supreme ecclesial authority him who denied his Lord three times? In Peter it becomes fundamentally evident that mission and person are timelessly identical only in Christ; thus, in him alone are the priest who offers and the lamb being offered identical. But two things are given Peter at his installation in office: the command "follow me" (containing the grace needed for following) and the rich promise of "the kind of death by which he would glorify God", that is, by a literal, though reverse, mirror-image, crucifixion, by which the ecclesial office is really drawn into the Lord's most primordial authority. Paul's concluding words to the Corinthians hold good for the entire office supremely embodied by Peter: "You require proof that Christ is speaking in me; he is not weak toward you, but powerful *in* you. He was in fact crucified through weakness, but he lives by God's power. We too are weak in him, but toward you we shall show ourselves very much alive in him by God's power" (2 Cor 13:3f.).

Hence, the one commanding may not anxiously measure the authenticity of his claim to authority by his personal witness, notwithstanding the fact that he must also strive for the authenticity of this witness. The synthesis of authority and witness cannot be institutionalized; therefore, ecclesial obedience cannot depend on the degree of this synthesis. The same is true in the purely human sphere: there is official authority (that of a judge, public servant or government official) and there is personal authority, based on knowledge, ability, maturity; the community cannot be dependent on the attained identity of both. That this is valid in the Church is one of Augustine's central, lasting insights against the Donatists. The secular analogy ought not to make it impossible for those outside the Church to have at least some presentiment of the mystery of ecclesial obedience; of course, it will become clear only when one considers that ecclesial obedience in its entirety—as personal obedience to God, as communal and as official obedience—stands under the sign of discipleship to the Crucified.

This will become clearer still in our third and final section, where we shall more closely examine the relation between general ecclesial obedience and religious obedience, since the latter can be nothing but an elucidation and intensification of certain elements of ecclesial obedience.

Here it is not possible to distinguish specifically clerical obedience from specifically religious obedience. Both are determined by characteristics of the evangelical counsels, as can be clearly seen time and again in Church history up to the Middle Ages and even beyond, and finally in all the encyclicals on the priesthood issued by recent popes. Though the various missions—of the priest, religious, lay person in a secular institute—may make for a variety of nuances in the concrete expressions of religious life, in their fundamental orientation they are all subject to the same norm: that of following Christ as closely as possible, even in his obedience.

3. Ecclesial Obedience and Obedience in Religious Life

Every form of religious life in the Church originates from the desire, and still more from the calling, of individual persons and groups in the Church to take Jesus' call to follow him more literally than is possible to most other Christians and to work earnestly at identifying their entire life with Jesus' invitation to live in and from his life. Thus it is not the intention of religious life to found a "special" Church alongside the so-called "general Church", but rather to endeavor to authenticate the Church's nature as the body of Christ.

The three evangelical counsels (whose historical development will not be treated here) are not three juxtaposed entities; they are rather the anthropologically necessary, threefold expression of a *single* disposition of total disponibility for discipleship within the christological mission.

As a possibility within the Church, this way of life obviously shares first of all in all the forms and tensions mentioned in the first two sections. It is "advertised" in the original calling of the disciples in the Gospels and again very expressly in the first Christian community in Jerusalem, as well as—according to Paul's testimony (2 Cor 8–9)—elsewhere also. It unfolds in the three dimensions indicated: in the immediacy of each individual to the triune God; in the community of all Christ's members, who serve and obey one another with their charisms; and in the submission to an authority that mediates this immediacy and community.

Since here, however, we are immediately interested in the counsel of obedience and not in the counsels to leave everything and to observe celibacy, we shall investigate the relationship between Church authority and the competent authority for religious life. In this area there is the possibility of their being identical or to a large extent not identical.

For the priest, who promises obedience to his bishop, there is identity in a far more intensive sense than for the laity of the diocese. Identity can also occur in the case of a secular institute that has no other superior except the local bishop, to whose directives regarding dedication to work and matters of conscience the member submits.

But extensive non-identity prevails where an order or congregation elects its own abbot or superior general and other officials and, as a practice in following Christ more closely, freely submits to the authority given them. Something of this kind can take place only within the hierarchical Church, with its approbation of this way of life as one conducive to Christian perfection; whereas in the Church, the authority of the pope and of the bishop with his priests is instituted by Christ and never exists because of the good pleasure of the Church's members, who can elect a superior but not ordain him.

To a certain limited degree, a community within the Church can call itself a "model of the universal Church": for instance, insofar as a Benedictine abbey with its Rule, its abbot, its schedule of prayer and work and the humility and self-renunciation of its monks can become a city on the hill, visible from afar off to the people of God living around it; or the mendicant orders or the Society of Jesus can represent in the Church the leaven which the Church, as the power of God's kingdom in the world, should form, and so forth. But the ideality thus set up is not above the Church or for her, but—in proportion to its success—in her, of her very self.

The counsel of obedience is embraced because of a special, personal call to follow Christ. In the gospel, not everyone is called to this closer following, as can be seen in the example of the man healed at Gerasa, whose request to join the Lord and his disciples is refused. This call claims the entire existence of the one called—"leave everything"—in order to put on, as Paul says, the form of Jesus' obedience definitively and in incarnative fashion. An important feature of such a call is that it is always made by name, in personal solitude, never in groups, though for each person (even for the hermit) it is of course a call into the ecclesial community. The surrender of one's existence to Jesus, and through him to the Father in the Spirit, is unconditional and absolute, although the choice of the means of living out this absoluteness—for instance, to enter *this* particular Order—remains relative, that is, related to this absoluteness.

With this, the first aspect of religious obedience becomes evident: the choice of a superior capable of giving the person called a spiritual leadership that will train him in absolute obedience to God. For the person called, this superior is an expert in the spiritual life and all its difficulties, a *pneumatikós* around whom the first desert monks flocked, a *starets*. However, as soon as the second essential dimension of obedience is added—the community (*koinōnia*) of mutual obedience in love—in which the person called must be immediately exercised as an ecclesial person, the function of the pneumatic leader simultaneously becomes that of superior of the community. This superior is chosen *by* the community, not merely on the basis of his enlightened ability to guide the individual but also because of his prudence that qualifies him for the office of head of the community. Possibly the functions in an order will be differentiated: here, the novice master and the so-called *pater spiritualis*; there, the superior of the house, of the province, and so on. Such matters remain incidental and do not affect the counsel of obedience. Only let it be noted that no pneumatic person, even though called to found an order, can claim any ecclesial authority; nor has any founder approved by the Church ever done so. (In this regard, the *regula magistri* constitutes a delicate borderline case.)

The first dimension of the counsel of obedience (the call to personal immediacy to Christ's obedience) cannot and may not gain ascendency over the second (obedience in ecclesial mutuality) in such a way that the practice of *agape* becomes a means to the end of gnostic, solitary perfection (as is the case with Evagrius Ponticus). What Evagrius calls *praktikē* may never be allowed to descend to a preliminary stage of (mystical) knowledge of God, since, according to Paul, Christian *agape* is the goal and summit of all personal charisms. The cenobitic life is not a preliminary step toward the eremitical life; once he has become perfect in love of neighbor, the truly Catholic hermit lives eminently in and for the communion of saints, as the Carmelite ideal clearly demonstrates. Prevalent nowadays is the opposite danger: that the communal dimension of the counsel of obedience may predominate over the personal element. This may be carried so far that the community democratically decides and votes on everything to be done or changed, with the result that the fundamental christological and crucifying dimension is often almost or completely lost. The community chapter advises, but the abbot decides: certainly after having listened to the opinion of all, including the youngest brother, with utmost seriousness and most profound humility. Where the community as such claims for itself permanent highest authority, the calling of the individual is frustrated and the field of the religious life has been abandoned.

Nor can the counsel of obedience ever outgrow

the third dimension: ecclesial, hierarchical obedience. Francis of Assisi lays his Rule at the pope's feet; Ignatius takes the pope as highest superior of his order. Juridical exemption means release from certain restricting bonds (to the local bishop) in order to be bound more immediately to the interests of the Church on a universal scale. Nowadays, however, whether and to what extent such release actually serves these interests is frequently questioned. Provision is still made for secular institutes to receive diocesan approbation; but the bishop may not requisition them for diocesan purposes.

The three-dimensional counsel of obedience can assume any number of nuances, but it cannot dispense with any of its dimensions if it is to remain a way of life within the Catholic Church. It may not become one-sidedly personal (religious life for the sake of "personal perfection"), nor one-sidedly social or prone to group dynamics (as in certain pentecostal groups), nor one-sidedly functional in favor of the hierarchy (as Ignatian obedience is sometimes portrayed in caricature). As a whole it must be classified as a charism, but nowadays one has to guard against Donatist tendencies. The Donatist judges the priest or charismatic leader on the basis of his degree of spiritual endowment and, accordingly, obeys him more or less, completely or not at all; in the end, therefore, he obeys his own inspired judgment, which amounts to no obedience whatever.

In a period influenced by the so-called history of freedom since the Enlightenment, this kind of Donatism is in the Christian's blood also. At best one obeys the person whose spiritual authority is obvious—one who is authority, not one who has it. Two things are forgotten: that all human authority in the Church has the character of a sign pointing to God, to Christ, to the gospel, to the ideality of the *ecclesia immaculata infallibilis*; and that ecclesial authority is primarily a founded authority, not a self-assumed one, however much its bearer has to try as far as possible to shape his life so as to witness to the authority entrusted to him. But, a priori, no history of freedom can develop beyond Christ's authority and the duty to point to it and the *exousia* to represent it. For there is no greater freedom than God's, even though the Son's freedom in God consists in always doing the Father's will out of the fullness of divine love; in always revealing, not himself, but the Father's love; in always regarding his own fullness in the Spirit as the Father's gift. This gift enables him, as man, to obey the Father more humbly and, as God and as glorified God-man, to breathe out into the Church and the world, together with the Father, this Spirit of freedom and no other.

FRAGMENTS ON
SUFFERING AND HEALING

"Onward with Rigorous Fighting"

Only the person who takes the world as it is has a
chance to think and say something admissible
about it, even if the first thing he says is that it
must be changed because it is unbearable as it is. It
is absolutely pointless to speculate about other
possible (better or worse) worlds.

What exists? A humanity propagating itself and
leaving its dead behind, doing battle for millenia
with the powers of the cosmos: powers that in
part must be controlled if mankind is to live and in
part are uncontrollable, as the advancing glaciers
were for people of the Ice Age and the earthquake
is in our own day. The trodden anthill must be
completely rebuilt.

The enemy is not only without; he is within
man. His psyche and his organism flourish only in
a temperate zone between extremes that would
destroy him: not only too little but also too much
pleasure and joy turn into suffering. At most, the
species can bother about sick or dying individuals
incidentally, for it has to see to its own survival.
What is of even more consequence is that when

humanity has achieved something in one branch, this perfected specialty threatens to put itself in the wrong; relative to the whole and the average, it proves to be "decadent" and ends up in a biological impasse or is killed by the stronger ones. In view of this mechanism, a state of combat seems to be more important for humanity than the attainment of even a merely relatively peaceful existence.

When Johannes Tepl complains about the hideousness, horror and injustice of death, which has robbed him of his beloved wife, Death sneers back at him:

> If since the time of the first man formed from clay we had not thinned out the overgrowth and propagation of people on earth, and of animals and worms, the swarm of tiny mosquitoes alone would make life impossible; no one would dare to go outside for fear of the wolves; one man would devour the other for lack of food; there would not be enough room on earth for everyone. Anyone mourning the death of a mortal is a fool![1]

Humanity seems to need a total threat on every front in order to stay fit for battle: where demons of nature no longer threaten primitive man nor the

[1] Johannes von Tepl, *Der Ackermann und der Tod* (Inselbücherei, 1981), 12f.

257

envy of the gods the ancient cultures, modern man builds atom bombs for himself so that he can live in the fear of death.

To want procreation is to want death, too, and all its trappings. Qoheleth knew this in his day: "There is a time for giving birth and a time for dying" (3:2).

Long before Schopenhauer and Darwin, the cosmos was recognized as an "eternally ruminating monster"; nonsolidarity with it and escape from it, along with various practices for making oneself insensitive, were recommended as a way to salvation. Those who can treat themselves to this way abandon the society of their suffering fellow human beings or make themselves immune to their sufferings. Such self-healings will never bring healing to the world; however much courage they may require of an individual, he still remains a coward in the face of reality.

To bank one's entire destiny on reincarnations is certainly not a means of slowly working oneself out of the suffering world, not even when one has recognized suicide as an unacceptable means of doing so. On the contrary, those thinkers are right who see in the perspective of death as the temporal end of an unrepeatable, temporal life the necessary prerequisite for moral acts that engage a person's entire existence and demand decisions not revocable at will.

If this is true, then the dignity of the human person is inseparable from death (and all its mental and physical harbingers). To say Yes and Amen to the human being as a fighter in the cosmos is likewise to affirm those who are suffering and dying. "From the Christian viewpoint, to affirm suffering is a part of the overall Yes and not, as it may sometimes appear, the only thing and the decisive thing behind which the affirmation of life completely disappears."[2]

Therefore,

"Onward with rigorous fighting", as an old Brandenburger margrave of the Reformation put it. For in the end we all suffer so deeply that we can hold out only by battling vigorously, sword in hand. And since we want nothing at all for *ourselves* and can joyfully and with good conscience expose ourselves to the most severe strife, we should call out to one another, "Only the soldier is a free man"; and anyone who wants to be, remain or become a free person has no other choice: "Onward with rigorous fighting."[3]

[2] Dorothee Sölle, *Leiden* (Stuttgart and Berlin: Kreuzverlag, 1973), 136.

[3] Friedrich Nietzsche, *Briefe* (Berlin: Schuster & Loeffler, 1900–1901) vol. 1, 352.

According to what we have said, one need not
view things solely on the biological level in a
Darwinian way—only the strong individuals and
species survive and see to it that the weak disappear, if they do not perish of themselves. Rather,
one can find the laws of the lower world sub-
limated in the higher. In the realistic world, which
is the only one that exists, no one becomes strong
without painful inurement, no one noble without
a thousand renunciations and self-inflicted wounds,
no one a true artist without remaining unrecognized for a long time and, in all probability, after a
tragic life (one has only to read Walter Muschg);
and certainly no one becomes a saint without
appropriate participation in the Cross. Portmann's
extra-uterine year is significant: the human being
is expelled too early from the security of the
womb (according to Freud, the only really blessed
state) into the world of anxious cravings (read
"libido" in a buddhist sense for once!). The Greek
play on words *pathei manthanein*, to learn by suffering, proves true in everyone.

Only by choosing can a person become free at
all; and anyone who has a choice also has anguish,
for he must leave aside something desirable. In his
most renowned and contested work, de Lubac has

shown that God could not create any angel or any human being in a definitive state of good from the outset: the spiritual being himself must decide what ought to be best for him. One could object that the act of renouncing oneself as ultimate goal and preferring God takes place in a kind of ecstasy of love, painlessly. But one should see to it that everything resembling inner coercion and vanquishment is excluded from this ecstasy. "Anyone who loves his life will lose it": this is valid even for the very first choice of the spiritual creature. If he is to be free, he cannot be spared this "suffering".

It is superfluous to itemize all the feats of the taskmaster called suffering: from the infant that is weaned and has to learn that even wailing does not get him what he wants, through the unavoidable suffering of every school child, of everyone standing before tests, of everyone making a living at a hated job, to the numberless illnesses that train and mature us, teach us patience and foster understanding for the suffering of others, heal our addictions and open up a realm of inner treasures to replace our outer pleasures. An extreme example of this is Jacques Lusseyran, who, having become blind as a boy, found the strength to discover an inner light and to develop an eye for it. In the hell of Buchenwald concentration camp, this inner light finally led him to become the guide of innumerable people.[4]

Normally the moral development of a person takes place in two stages. In the first, his spiritual freedom learns to overcome the sensual enticements of the physical world around him. This process of overcoming, painful and joyful[5] at the same time, is its own reward. In the second and final stage, the powers of nature become overpowering in terminal illness and death; but in its diminution the spirit can still triumph, as tragedy, especially idealistic tragedy, shows. Sufferings gave Mary Stuart the maturity needed to die her outstanding death.

> Only intense pain is the final liberator of the spirit. . . . That long, slow pain which takes its time, in which we are burned as it were with green wood, forces us . . . to go down to our deepest depths and to cast off every trust and everything easygoing, feigned, indulgent and middling in

[4] *Das wiedergefundene Licht*, 2nd ed., Siebenstern 155 (Hamburg, 1971).

[5] Language indicates the fluidity between joy and sorrow. In German, *ge-winnen* (to win) and *über-win(d)en* (to overcome) show that the Old High German and Germanic *winnan* (to struggle, to obtain by hard fighting) is derived from the same root as Old High German *wini* (friend, as desired and won) and *wunni* (delight).

which we have perhaps heretofore invested our humanity.[6]

Here the tragic advocate of "Yes and Amen" wants to compete with the Christian.

Life itself, its eternal fruitfulness and recurrence, conditions the torment, the destruction, the will to annihilation. . . . One finds that the problem is one of the meaning of suffering, whether a Christian meaning or a tragic one. In the former it is supposed to be the way to a state of holiness; in the latter, the state of existence is regarded as holy enough to justify even an immense amount of suffering. The tragic person affirms even the harshest suffering: he is strong, full and deifying enough for that.[7]

It so happened that the one who said this broke on his affirmation and "divinity". However, one could also formulate the alternative differently by presenting Jesus himself as the one who affirms suffering to the point of his own destruction (and see his equality with God therein[8]) and let those who looked upon the Cross vow to commit themselves to change society in such a way that no one would ever again be crushed by suffering: "Love

[6] Nietzsche, *Die fröhliche Wissenschaft*, Preface, 3.
[7] Ibid., *Nachlass* (Schlecta III, 773).
[8] Sölle, *Leiden*, 172.

263

cannot resign itself to the senselessness of suffering and destruction. . . . Not withdrawal from
the problem but its solution is necessary."[9] This
is not the anti-Christian but the post-Christian
solution, which upgrades the healing power of
suffering to the absolute.

The change perceptible here arises when Christian healing by virtue of Jesus' Cross is linked
with the idea that suffering can to a large extent
be done away with, an idea launched by modern
technology—hypnosis, surgery, analysis, medicine
in general, but also sociology and worldwide
industry. Christianity has opened its eyes to the
injustice in the world that cries to heaven for
vengeance, but apparently it has not done enough
to eliminate that injustice. The post-Christians
set out to do so; their suffering at the sight of
the world's suffering impels them to draft a new
gospel according to which man's battle with cosmic powers enters into a new phase. And some
Christians think that they ought to bring the old
gospel of redemptive suffering to focus completely
on the new one of liberation from suffering.

Teilhard de Chardin was sensible enough to
unite both truths. In the first phase there is an
active struggle against suffering, that caused by

[9] Ibid., 177.

social injustice as well as against that which is purely physical; nor does he fail to mention that a struggling humanity always has to undertake great renunciations in order to pursue its goal.[10] But man is fighting against a superpower, like Jacob with the God-angel. Nevertheless, precisely because in the active battle against suffering he has grown as a sufferer, he now has "the ardent courage to die into another".[11] His "passivities" or capacities to suffer have been purified by effective healing, so that his self-surrender in suffering, his weakness, his dying become a (mysteriously hidden) fruitful "act" of love, of affirmation of the absolute Being that overpowers him. Anyone who thus suffers God's will in dying is still *doing* God's will. The space that he, as fighter against suffering, has made free within himself is not an area of passive, stoic resignation; it is a zone of love for the humanly impossible, which is the divine Possible, God himself.

But did Teilhard's fervent soul sufficiently consider that the first, active phase only leads to the inevitable threshold of the second if it has already acted in the spirit of the second, in readiness for self-giving and for receiving? And is God not free

[10] *Le Milieu Divin*, *Oeuvres* vol. 4 (1975), 63: "Le Détachement par l'action".
[11] Ibid., 71.

to send a person insuperable suffering—small, greater, greatest—even in the current phase of his activity, suffering that is ultimately incomprehensible, as in the testing of Abraham or Job? Many accusations have been advanced against the sadistic God of the Moriah episode, who demands back the very thing to which he had attached the most solemn promise and torments to the quick the father of the child to be offered up. But in the question of this and analogous severe tests of faith, is it not meaningful that Abraham's faith, till now hidden in his soul, potential, ready, still untested in its soundness, be actuated—as, for example, Mary's readiness was actuated at the foot of the Cross—when it is a matter of proving him to be the sound bridge over which an entire people will march and on whose handrails it will have to find support? Nevertheless, when it comes to Job's humanly immeasurable trial, it can only be interpreted—unknown to him—by looking ahead to the absolute suffering of the absolutely innocent one. This suffering earns for God and the world a fruitfulness infinitely surpassing every possible fruit of human activity and at the same time incapable of being authentically counterposed to activity. In view of the Cross, Job's suffering, which defies any attempt to heal and to comfort, is healing in a sense inaccessible to Job (as it was to Jesus himself), as the mysterious songs of the

"Servant of God" say of him who "has borne our infirmities and carried our sorrows; but we thought of him as punished, stricken by God and afflicted" (Is 53:4).

We have been speaking of salutary suffering, of the pedagogue indispensable in the school of real life, which teaches us to endure and to transcend, even when in the end we are inevitably overcome physically. With all his crying out for justice, his "praying revolt",[12] Job belongs to those who, crushed by suffering, stand firm as the "just", without being aware of it (in the end he is the only one justified by God), like Jesus, who cries out his godforsakenness on the Cross and is justified by God on Easter. Beyond all possible healing, these just ones pass over to the side of those who heal.

At the end of this train of thought, however, we must ask: why does the only one who could prevent or heal horror hide himself at this point? Why does he appear only in the distorted mask of the sadist—as those tormented to death must regard him, completely oppressed as they are? This will be our final question, but before that, there is one thing more to be said: if the Christian "answer" (insofar as one can call it that) refers to

[12] E. Zenger and R. Böswald, *Durchkreuztes Leben: Besinnung auf Hiob* (Herder, 1976), 26. Zenger's opinions regarding Job's situation are, however, not altogether balanced and are evidently influenced in part by D. Sölle's statements.

the Trinity, then it does not do so as though the Father (as the "Lord" God) were mercilessly to abandon the divine Son, as the crushed human worm, to suffering (leaving us in a quandary as to where the Holy Spirit fits in).[13] For the triune God does not consist of three gods; rather, one single trinitarian resolution of healing will is carried out in the same freedom, love and self-giving, in the same Holy Spirit. Whether this warrants speaking of a suffering God is still to be decided.[14] For the time being, one conclusion is to be borne in mind: that the one suffering and the one concurring in that suffering—who is also the healer—are one, fulfilling their task in one single common Spirit.

Healing

If man is a fighter against cosmic (super-) powers and here and there wins a piece of territory from the enemy, then the ability to restrain suffering by his own power belongs to his nature, whether he does it with psychic means (cf. the countless

[13] J. Moltmann, *The Crucified God: The Cross of Christ as the Foundation and Criticism of Christian Theology* (London: SCM Press, 1974).

[14] K. Kitamori, *Theologie des Schmerzes Gottes* (Göttingen: Vandenhoeck & Ruprecht, 1972); François Varillon, *La Souffrance de Dieu* (Paris: Centurion, 1975). Cf. Peter Kuhn, *Gottes Selbsterniedrigung in der Theologie der Rabbinen* (Munich: Kösel, 1967); Jean Galot, *Dieu souffre-t-il?* (Lethielleux, 1976).

"books of consolation" of antiquity and of the Middle Ages) or with technical means, such as medicine, surgery, narcotics or psychotherapy. But already here, as a reverberation of what we have just said, we should note two things. The sufferer, whether suffering primarily mentally or physically, is always a single person; the spirit affects the body and the body the spirit. Thus primitive medicine was always integral: the medicine man was and is both physician and priest. And although the two functions became differentiated in time, they converge again and again, at least in the sense that they work closely together: for instance, a psychotherapist with a spiritual director (in case they cannot be combined in one person). Gion Condrau says of the therapist that he can heal only by means of an inner, loving interest in the patient; notwithstanding his technical superiority and role as guide, he must meet the patient with an unconditional love[15] and in the

---

Other literature in A. Feuillet, *L'Agonie de Gethsémani* (Gabalda, 1977), 258–59.

[15] Gion Condrau, "Wesen und Bedeutung der Psychotherapie" in J. Rudin, *Neurose und Religion* (Walter Olten, 1964), 20, 47: "In the unconditionality of the physician's kindness and love lies the secret of psychotherapeutic treatment. . . . In psychotherapy a person often experiences for the first time that love is genuine love only when no conditions are attached to it."

healing process "include the spiritual welfare of the human being . . . for are not we modern physicians all descendants of the ancient priestly doctors?"[16] This holds good for all physicians, as also for all surgeons, whose dedication and self-conquest often reach superhuman heights and toward whom patients generally acquire a deeply human relationship of trust and gratitude.

What is valid for the doctor who heals by means of natural skill coupled with human dedication is correspondingly true of every helper and especially every consoler. Such a person can render assistance with an innate talent, but will never be effective without true sacrificial self-dedication. Presupposing this, everyone can become his neighbor's therapist. (The reason why Job's friends did not function as such for the sufferer lies ultimately in their lack of dedication, in their know-it-all attitude that seeks to console on the basis of preconceived theories rather than of the meaning inherent in the sufferer himself.)

Applied to the domain of grace, this natural law assumes a new depth: a sufferer is healed only in the participatory suffering (com-passion) of the healer. Jesus, who becomes the healer of the hemorrhaging woman, knows when he is touched

[16] Ibid., 56.

"that power had gone out of him" (Mk 5:30; Lk 8:46). This loss of strength in a healer reaches all the way from natural experience—for instance, that of a physiotherapist—through that of a guru up to the completely supernaturalized Jesus, who draws his miraculous powers in advance from the reserve of total com-passion with all sufferers that he will experience on the Cross. Not without reason does he call his mother's attention to his "hour", the Cross, on the occasion of his first miracle at Cana: the transformation he now effects is only a foretoken of the one definitive transformation of all suffering in his approaching desolation.

One can speak of a genuine healing when a sufferer who was previously the slave of his suffering becomes its master, accepts it in inner freedom and, if he is a Christian, lets God manage and allot it. This opens up a very far-reaching subject that we can merely hint at in a few words:[17] the manifold simultaneity of suffering and joy in the soul. There is not only such a thing as superficial joy amid excruciating suffering and superficial pain amid inner peace or even joy; one can experience joy in a purifying suffering also (in the smarting

[17] On this subject, see "Die Freude und das Kreuz" in *Die Wahrheit ist symphonisch* (Einsiedeln: Johannes Verlag, 1972) 131–46.

271

pain of a shameful confession as in the painful lancing of an abscess). The Pauline distinction between "godly grief" that leads to salvation and "worldly grief" that produces death has a place here (2 Cor 7:8ff.). And who but God alone can know whether, in the very depths of the suffering, pain-benighted soul, this suffering is not after all accepted?

This dialectic corresponds to a similar one in the healer. How deep is his readiness to receive and meet the sufferer where he is suffering most deeply? Will he prematurely withdraw from solidarity with the sufferer, or is he ready to accompany him to the end, if necessary? Will he rely on his technique alone or will he root his technique in his existence? Will he habitually be ready to show interest in the chance and unexpected sufferer, or will he specialize in certain cases and encapsulate himself against the rest? Every newspaper we open places us before this question of conscience. We are not in a position to cope with the flood of suffering of every kind spread out before us in the papers; but if we had the means, would we be ready to contribute to its healing as much as we possibly could, or has our affluent world provided us with protection like a duck's feathers so that unpleasantness "rolls off"?

If as possible healers we are open to others,

then whether or not we are equipped with special therapeutic powers is unimportant. Our readiness to share in suffering, to let ourselves be affected—not masochistically, but in a perfectly sober and realistic fashion, accepting the world as it presents itself—is essentially healing, whether it is actually exercised or only potentially offered. Even in the natural sphere, people with such readiness are the refuge of all sufferers; this is true all the more and with an infinitely increased fruitfulness in the supernatural sphere. Jesus Christ founded the one "religion" that in no way attempts to circumvent suffering and pain, to overstep or to eradicate them (which is impossible); instead, it faces the world's horror in an attitude that revalues it and changes it more profoundly than do all the episodic, violent revolutions—however necessary they may be—designed to abolish the most flagrant injustice.

Approaches to Final Healing

Sorrow and suffering are so deeply entrenched in our cosmos that we cannot even imagine a world without them. Long before there were any human beings, the animals were preying on one another. One could advance the hypothesis that the material

273

cosmos was caused by a primary revolt of the spiritual powers commanding the cosmos; but biblical revelation casts insufficient light on this area, in which research is of no practical help.[18] At the most, we can imagine a world in which there exists something like pain without its having degenerated into suffering: pain occasioned by the resistance that other finite freedoms in their sphere of the world offer to my freedom in my sphere of the world. This resistance of the freedoms among themselves would have to be settled without the one overpowering the other.

From this point we could look to the world's divine prototype, in the Christian understanding of which three hypostases consubstantially possess one divine freedom and wisdom. It is not that one of them (the Father) imperiously overwhelms the others; rather, in the *contra* and *con* of their relationships, one divine decree results. And—in a sense hardly comprehensible to us—one might say that each hypostasis "suffers" the will of the

[18] C. S. Lewis in his very instructive book *The Problem of Pain* (London, 1940) distinguishes between pain—a given in every material environment which, however, need not amount to actual suffering—and the disorder existing in nature even before the appearance of man, which he tentatively attributes to a disruption of nature caused by the fall of the angels.

others. If on earth the incarnate Son unequivocally does the Father's will presented to him by the Holy Spirit, then in eternity a stupendous, free offering of self by the Son to the Father must have preceded this obedience. This offer of the Son to stand up for the well-being of the world with his own blood and his anguish must have touched the depths of the Father's heart. Since it was the best possible offer and the supreme revelation of absolute love, the Father could only agree to it—with "bleeding heart" (to continue using anthropomorphic terms).

This would mean two things. First of all, we can simply discard all the images of God that represent the Father as a sadistic tyrant from whom the suffering Son has finally freed us because the suffering servant is greater than the afflicting Lord, whether these images be presented by Marx or Bloch or D. Sölle or C. G. Jung (in his book on Job). And we will refrain from projecting such a notion back onto Anselm's teaching on the redemption, for he knows very well that everything was set in motion by trinitarian love, especially the Father's love.

Regarding this point, let it be noted that complaints against God, heroic rebellions and *hommes revoltés* are a biblical and post-biblical invention that would never have occurred to a devout heathen.

275

(I am not referring to myths about battles among the gods and the vanquishing of old generations of gods by new ones, but to revolt against the "supreme good", against "Being itself".) Every good ancient philosophy, whether Chinese, Indian or Greek, would have labelled such a revolt sheer stupidity; the identity of absolute essential power and absolute truth and wisdom was only too evident to this kind of thinking. And this in the face of the undiminished problem of suffering in the world, for which other causes can be blamed. Even mythologizing Gnosis, which suffered enough from evil in the world, never presumed to make the supreme God responsible for it. A complaining attitude toward the Absolute becomes possible only where one pictures God as a finite, limited "Lord" of the suffering world (whose divinity on that account loses its credibility and degenerates into a phantom for atheists). Regardless of the intensity of Job's suffering, he *must* be reduced to silence by the Absolute, whose power and wisdom coincide. But although this omnipotence is no "argument" in the eyes of the reasoner, the attitude of the triune God in view of him who hangs on Golgotha, "having been made a curse", will serve as one. This brings us to our second point.

The loving in one another of the freedom of

the divine hypostases—whose oppositeness becomes sufficiently clear in the Incarnation—is not
a mere gentle light; it is "glory" as blazing fire.
"Love is strong as death; jealousy is cruel as the
grave. Its flashes are flashes of fire, a flame from
Yahweh" (Song 8:6f.). "God is a consuming fire"
(Dt 9:3; Heb 12:29). If we are one day to live in
God, we must become like the salamanders of
legend: creatures who have become so used to
this fire that they can stand it. Is it any wonder
that, in creating the finite, this fire begins by
separating into pleasure and pain—correlative,
mutually requisite poles? And this before the resistance offered by finite freedom embitters this correlation into suffering and finally into the terrible
state that Simone Weil calls "*malheur*" (misfortune,
woe). The divine fire needs fuel that it can transform, purify and transfigure into effulgent bodies.
Whether sinful or not, the finite must somehow or
other die into God, surrender its "for-itself" in
order to live in the only ultimate "in-itself"; and
this transition—ecstasy, burning, death—will be
pain, or at least something analogous to pain.

Accordingly, we read in the writings of all the
mystics that *God's fire wounds by healing and heals by
wounding*, that, in this regard, being wounded and
being healed are one and the same thing, that
ascent into heaven is unthinkable without descent

into hell: "He afflicts and shows mercy; he leads down to the underworld and up again, and no one can escape his hand" (Tob 13:2; Dt 32:39; 1 Sam 2:6; Wis 16:13, 15). Therefore Augustine can praise God "through whom the universe, even with its sinister side, is perfect . . . by whose decree the utmost dissonance is nil, since what is less perfect is in harmony with what is more perfect" (Solil. I, 1, 2). This is not meant in a pantheistic sense; it acquires its full meaning only in the light of the Trinity. For creation, with its danger and antimony, became possible only through the eternal Son's offer to transform the most wicked world into the "very good", the best world by the fire of his loving Passion. Creation burns in divine fire that changes all rebellion into suffering and holds the fire of purification in the Cross ready for all suffering, in order thus to contain the contradiction in healing. A free entity that refused to be purified by God's fire would have to suffer eternally in itself from the inescapable divine fire.

Nowadays we speak all too readily of God's suffering at the pain of his creation, as though only such talk could exonerate him. We also speak too readily of God's mutability. We consider too little that the fire of God's eternal love is exalted far above the finite things that we call pleasure and

278

suffering, just as his vitality is exalted far above what we contrapose as "being" and "becoming".

In the end it is unimportant that, in this world as it is, we cannot make a clear-cut distinction between pain that comes from God and pain that is caused by the fault of creatures. What encompasses both and continues to give everything meaning is the unique Cross of the Son—his triune Cross, let us say—in whose purifying fire suffering and healing are one.

In a static sense, the suffering of this world may be as heavy as it will; in view of this fire one must say: "Our momentary light distress is effecting an eternal weight of glory beyond all measure, since we are not keeping our eyes on things visible, but on things invisible; for what is visible is transient, but what is invisible is eternal" (2 Cor 3:17ff.).

MARTYRDOM AND MISSION

Considering the immense sea of suffering that people have inflicted on one another in the history of the world—murders of individuals and entire peoples, tortures of every kind such as only the perverse human brain can concoct, planned mass exterminations—it is not easy to single out the atrocities perpetrated against Christians in the last two thousand years. Is there any sense in making them the subject of a separate consideration? After all, countless other so-called innocent people have likewise been killed on account of their religious, political or moral convictions; or simply because they were in the way of someone powerful, a tyrant or an expansion-needy race or people; or because they represented an alien element in their environment, such as the Jews in Egypt or Persia, who long before the Christian era were persecuted and partially exterminated in organized massacres.

The time of Nero to that of Diocletian was marked by heroic spiritual courage in countless people throughout the Roman Empire. Many had to submit to diabolically ingenious tortures. The rest were subject to ostracism at every level of society—high officials and residents of the imperial palaces as well as soldiers, merchants, the common people. Life in the catacombs was accompanied by the steadily gnawing fear of discovery and of betrayal by the always numerous informers, fear as to whether the impending tortures could be borne. And how many (as we know!) became weak with this fear and defected to offer the required sacrifice before the emperor's statue, often enough furtively and through back doors, in an effort to relieve their conscience artificially so that their left hand did not know what their right hand was doing. Assuming that we were to find sufficient reason to return in spirit to this heroic age of Christianity and make a special reflection on the many martyrdoms of this time, would not its entire edifying effect immediately be obliterated if we placed on the other side of the scale all the outrages committed by Christians (regardless of denomination) in every succeeding age, against those of other faiths—heretics or Jews, for example—and against fellow Christians? It is certainly dreadful to read that Emperor Galerius had his soldiers barricade and set on fire a Phrygian town whose inhabitants were all Christians, thus causing every man, woman and child to burn to death. But the illustrious builder of the Santa Sophia, the most Christian Emperor Justinian, did the same thing a number of times in order to eradicate certain sects, as well as the Jews, in Asia Minor. Nor was it any different during the Albigensian wars: the heretics were locked up in their churches and the churches set afire. Other highlights were the capture of Constantinople by the Crusaders, the conquest of Latin America by the Spanish, the Thirty Years' War, the Saint Bartholomew's Day Massacre, the living torches

281

of the Inquisition and the witch-hunts (comparable to those in Nero's gardens) and the executions of Savonarola and Giordano Bruno. There is no end of Christian abominations: they continue today in the tortures and prisons of South American military states, as well as in the hardheartedness of many Christian capitalist entrepreneurs who unscrupulously exploit poor peoples and nations.

It is not our intention here to denounce Christian history as having been especially cruel and bloody. We merely wish to ask whether it can be so clearly differentiated from the rest of the history of human atrocities that its martyrdoms need to be especially glorified vis-à-vis other martyrdoms, frequently enough caused by Christians. For instance, what if we were to consider without blinking the relations between Christians and Jews from the Middle Ages onward into modern times? Christians have suffered for their faith, as so many adherents of Islam and of other religions also have. But how intensely they have made the Jews suffer for their faith whenever they had the power to do so!

Where does all this lead us? In the first place, to the subdued conclusion that we ought to be very reserved and cautious regarding the cult of our martyrs and confessors, not on their account but on our own. If their suffering contains an element of glory, this glory is certainly not ours; it belongs solely to him for whom they suffered and died. Let us not adorn ourselves with finery—finery that belongs to God!

In this regard we might also keep in mind another point. We honor the faith-inspired courage of the martyrs, their total dedication to a cause that had nothing at all to offer them for their earthly existence. But, humanly speaking, they had no monopoly on that kind of courage. The Japanese who placed themselves in bombs in order to direct them to the right military targets and then explode with them likewise sacrificed themselves for a goal transcending their limited earthly existence—to mention but *one* example of such courage, of which ancient history also offers sufficient instances. And perhaps they do so more matter-of-factly and quietly than many a Christian would. In war, moreover, heroism is commonplace and does not call attention to itself. Medals of honor are bestowed (on the survivors!) almost incidentally. And how much unpretentious, unnoticed courage, even heroic courage unto death is exercised in everyday life, not only in oppressed countries where men, women and children have to struggle through from one day to the next but also in the slums of our affluent countries; in hospitals; in the lonely, seemingly meaningless

283

life of the elderly; in the martyrdom of unhappy marriages, in which people have to bear with one another without the support of love. No, in the immense anthill of humanity there is a prodigious amount of courage in the face of life and death. The Christian courage that makes martyrs certainly has a place here, but does it excel qualitatively to the extent that it is worthy of special notice? Take the epic of our century, *the* book that ought to survive even if all the others were to become extinct: Solzhenitsyn's *Gulag Archipelago*. There millions are gathered together not merely in the outer precincts of hell but even down in its very depths. And many are there because of the courage they exhibited before their arrest or have regained right in this hell. Only a fraction of them are wasting away here expressly on account of their Christian faith. For many others, it is because they rebelled against an existence unworthy of human beings and refused to sell their conscience, not wanting to bear the mark of the beast on their foreheads. And all these sufferers are in solidarity, imprisoned together by a regime that most certainly is rabidly anti-Christian but is no less anti-human, which is opposed to the elementary truth of humanity and, therefore, sold to every expedient lie. That is why the victims, Christian and humanist martyrs, are now confined in the same prison cells and sentenced to the same courage of resistance.

Let us suppose that the martyr for Christ's sake is still something special in relation to all these poor people, robbed of their human dignity. One thing, nevertheless, is given, or we might even say, gained: with his specialness, he is situated in a wonderful solidarity with all of humanity. He cannot claim any of that special veneration paid the martyrs by the early Church. Ultimately he is merely a person who has done his duty and adhered to his conscience and life decision on his Christian level, just as all his fellow sufferers have done on the common human level. It is true that nowadays the crowd still needs signs, monuments and memorials; but these could be called Scholl or Stauffenberg just as well as Delp or Bonhoeffer or Kolbe. And it is certainly still meaningful that individual countries, say of Africa or Asia, have their martyrs canonized to serve as special signals for the Christians' orientation and as intercessors whom they can invoke. But I scarcely think that the martyrs in their increasingly countless number, which is imperceptibly merging with the still more innumerable martyrs for humanity, can nowadays collectively attain to the renown of former times, and I certainly doubt that their bones can give rise to such a flourishing trade as in the Renaissance and Baroque periods.

I do not wish to speak now of the lamentable reasons why this is so: the incredible forgetfulness and indifference of modern people, even and especially in affluent countries, with respect to all the misery and all the heroic struggles in the world. Surfeited with news from the mass media, we scarcely notice even what is shocking: a slight shudder on reading the day's paper, perhaps a donation to the Red Cross, and tomorrow it will already be time for another shudder. When tens of thousands are frequently involved, does it matter if one black bishop simply "disappears" because of his faith? Deluged with all kinds of martyrdoms, we find it impossible to react to each one with any considerable emotion.

I would much rather go straight to the heart of the matter, to the true and decisive motive of Christian martyrdom, which today as ever distinguishes it from every other self-offering, however heroic. In the primitive Church, the martyrdoms were, as the word indicates, witnessings, but to a totally unique event that Paul expresses in an equally unique way: "I am crucified with Christ. I live; and yet it is no longer I, but Christ living in me. But what I am now living in the flesh, I live in faith in the Son of God who loved me and delivered himself up for me" (Gal 2:19–20). He is saying that there is one who, anticipating my existence, has suffered a martyrdom completely different from any that I or anyone else—even if he were Socrates—can suffer: a martyrdom for me, for my sake, in my place, vicariously for me who should have suffered it. Paul calls him "Christ", the anointed Messiah, and the "Son of God", who is obviously the only one empowered to die for the others, that is, for sinners (as is said elsewhere). The Christian really believes that his life is based on a vicarious death: not only his physical life but also his spiritual life, his life before God, the ultimate meaning of his existence. The Christian is indebted to another. And how else can he seriously acknowledge this debt than by following the same path as his Lord, since he has been very expressly invited to such discipleship and been just as expressly told in advance that the same thing will happen to the servant as to his master and to the pupil as to his teacher? This is the distinctive, special characteristic of the Christian martyr: he is "crucified with Christ", and the giving up of his life is an act of proper response, of self-evident gratitude. He does not die for an idea, even for the highest—not for human dignity, freedom or solidarity with the oppressed (though all of these may be included and play a role). He dies with someone who has died for him in advance.

What the early Christians loved and admired in their martyrs was this: that in giving their lives they were able to give a full, somehow humanly possible, adequate response to the deed of their Lord, who as the consubstantial Son of God possessed the competency and the power to deliver himself up for all, thus revealing the depths of the Father's heart, the sentiments of the divine origin. It is as though this clear response were to strike a balance that always remains unresolved with us who are eternally hesitating and bargaining. But some were really equal to it. They were able to solve the riddle put to all and win the prize. Or better, they knew the password and gained admission. On the way to martyrdom in Rome, the glorious Ignatius of Antioch entreats his Roman fellow Christians not to request his release:

> Have pity on me! I know what is good for me. Now I am beginning to be a disciple. Have pity on me, brothers! Do not debar me from life; do not wish death on me; do not hand over to the world him who wants to belong to God. Let me receive pure light. Allow me to imitate the suffering of my God (Rom 5:3–6:3).

This is not flight from the world but the passion of responsive love. A century later prudence is allowed to supervene. While many of his Christians must already give the witness of their lives, Bishop Cyprian goes into hiding and at first encourages them from the background not to be cowardly. Of course, his hour will soon strike, and his exemplary death will be flawless. One should not rush into martyrdom, for who knows what one still has to do for God in this life? But, equally, one may not refuse it when it is inevitably demanded. During the violent persecution of Decius, many recoiled, for instance by bribing the officials to issue certificates attesting that they had offered sacrifice. Who will be surprised at the great number of such people with two selves, when we must perceive how difficult it is in our day in communist countries to avoid being schizophrenic in some way or other, by making concessions to the regime that are apparently necessary for existence without intending to renounce the faith of one's heart? The persecutions of the first centuries generally flared up violently only for a short time and then merely smouldered underground. Nowadays, however, the basic hostility against Christians in communist states and in some nationalistic systems in Africa and Latin America is continuous. Hence, the temptation to come to terms with it is greater, and it is harder to draw the line between prudence and cowardice.

Though often misunderstood today, in antiquity the custom of survivors praying and celebrating the Eucharist on the tombs of the martyrs was very well understood. How could the intercession of those who had given the full response be other than powerful? It will not do to separate the idea of following Christ from that of imitating him (Paul also speaks of this) in such a way that the one crucified with Christ could not by grace obtain a share in Christ's redemptive work. Otherwise why would Jesus have invited his friends to follow him so closely and foretold for them persecution, rejection, court trials, even crucifixion (Jn 21)? This close bond between the follower and the "founder of our faith" (Heb 12:2) was fully familiar to the early Church. Paul himself speaks of filling up in his body what is still lacking to Christ's sufferings, that is, what Christ in mercy had reserved of his Cross in order to let his Church share in his work and suffering (Col 1:24).

The whole understanding of martyrdom in the primitive Church hinges on this mysterious parity —notwithstanding the disparity—between Christ and his Church, the Redeemer and those redeemed by him. The reasons for breaking down when faced with martyrdom may have been fear and cowardice, but not doubts about the truth of the faith. Later, after peace ensued under Constantine, when there was a vast influx of people into the Church, various christological heresies cropped up, and many Christians certainly possessed an insufficiently informed faith. Nevertheless (curiously enough, we may say), this Christian faith remained unassailable even then. The Church's official faith could be attacked from without, but not called into question from within. And there will always be those who die for this faith under dreadful torments, perhaps after having to defend it single-handedly, like the great Maximus the Confessor, against the superior strength of imperial edicts and of a clergy compliant because of cowardice.

Here, at the latest since the Enlightenment of the eighteenth century, an appalling change has taken place for us that deeply concerns our subject. What does the modern Christian believe regarding Christ's redemptive act? What does a great part of yesterday's Protestant and today's Catholic theology teach about it? Somewhat embarrassed, the lay person will perhaps admit that he does not know for sure. The idea of Christ's dying for my guilt vicariously before God seems so distant, so unverifiable! And on asking the theologians, we very often receive devious and evasive answers, answers in which, as on the continuous color chart, the meaning quite imperceptibly shades from a clear Yes to a clear No. There are many transitions. Let us cite a typical illustration. God, it is said, cannot undergo a change of mood—for instance, from an angry God into a reconciled God—on account of a mundane event. Consequently, even before Christ's Cross God was reconciled to the world and merely made this real disposition evident to mankind by means of the event of the Cross. The Cross is nothing more than a symbol of how much God loves the world, how much he is the Father, who, having always loved and watched for the lost son, runs to meet him and, forgiving everything, throws his arms around him. This means that in the godforsakenness of the Cross, in the hellish thirst of him who hung between heaven and earth and died with a loud cry, nothing happened that is essential for us. Furthermore, Cross and Eucharist are very intimately connected, for it is because Jesus gives his Body and Blood on the Cross *for* us that he can give it *to* us in the Eucharist. Hence, such a purely symbolic interpretation of the event on the Cross also debases the Last Supper to a symbolic commemorative meal of the Jesus who died centuries ago, a meal in which we recall in some vague manner God's graciousness to us and perhaps also his commandment of love.

The simple question that presents itself here is: Am I urged and obliged to give my life for such a symbol? And that perhaps in an extremely painful way, even by having to vegetate on its account for decades in a *gulag* under the most inhuman, humiliating circumstances? Who can require of me something that seems to lack any meaningful proportion? If a Russian scholar, not wanting to submit to the degrading demands of the regime, puts up with the concentration camp or the insane asylum instead, then the proportion is evident to anyone: it is a matter of witnessing with one's life to the dignity and truth of the human being and of appealing to the conscience of humanity as a whole. But when a Christian dares to risk the same thing for his faith in Christ, the world knows, if it hears of the fact and pays attention to it, that the Christian suffers or dies for something that he regards as the all-sustaining truth of his life, for something that, more profoundly than anything else, accounts for human dignity and human truth. Hence, a martyrdom that is not only humanistic, but beyond that truly Christian, witnesses to the unabridged, integral New Testament faith, whose core is the *pro nobis* of the Creed: "For us and for our salvation he became man; for us he was crucified, died and was buried." The Creed's remaining central declarations radiate from this core:

faith in Jesus' true, consubstantial divinity (which alone can overcome that insipid symbolism of which we just spoke); faith in the power of his sacramental representation; faith in his eschatological office of judge of the living and the dead; faith in the Holy Spirit, whom he won for us, and in eternal life, which he opened to us.

The genuine Christian martyr witnesses to this kind of world view. As Paul says, he "makes the good confession", in imitation of and conformity to his Lord, who was the first to have "made his noble profession before Pontius Pilate" (1 Tim 6:12f.). He can say, as Paul likewise says, "I know whom I have believed" (2 Tim 1:12). But what do they know who view the realism of the New Testament as naive, exaggerated, obsolete and urgently in need of demythologization? And for what could they die? They can hardly be called the light of the world and the salt of the earth, and Jesus tells us that if salt becomes insipid it is useless and can be thrown on the refuse heap. God has often used coarse instruments to get rid of what is good for nothing and make place for what is new and fruitful. What is caught up by the pitchfork and carried off—even if this included many thousands of stale, affluent Christians and a great many priests and religious who while away the time practising yoga and Zen—would all that be entitled to the great word "martyrdom"? I hardly think so. Fundamentally it is a matter of periodically cleaning up the spirit of the age so that world history can continue. That which no longer sounds the right tone cannot complain if it disappears in silence. And the people armed with pitchforks are very interested in having this "Christian" tone stop resounding in good time so that the cleanup can take place as inconspicuously as possible.

Of course, life on the dunghill can belatedly bring some people to their senses. The following quotation from a recent book serves to illustrate this:

> In prison, Bishop Schubert of Rumania, an authoritarian careerist, was addressed as "you fat pig", while the guard sneeringly poked him in his well-fed stomach. At this, the light suddenly dawned. In prison he became what countless meditations apparently had not helped him to be: the unfeigned brother of his ill-treated fellow prisoner. Innumerable examples illustrate such conversion to Christian brotherhood only and precisely in the forge of suffering.[1]

Such conversions are surely recorded in God's archives, and this brings us to another subject: the invisible and yet world-changing power of the

[1] Gerd Hamburger, *Verfolgte Christen* (Styria, 1977) 17.

suffering and silent Church, in which suffering purifies and deepens many, transforming them into true representatives of Christianity. This is the case even if the communications media take no note of it and perhaps very few of the Christians who are privileged to live in freedom think gratefully of this invisible representation before God. For it belongs indispensably to the substance of Christian faith to consider the fruitfulness of prayer and suffering for others as possible and real, and by no means to value it less than all the external undertakings that alter the structures of society. Drawing on the wisdom that life in East Germany can bestow, Heinz Schürmann has repeatedly appealed to our conscience in this regard. He says that just as Christ, God's final witness, knew when the hour of action and when the hour of endurance had struck, so too the Christian "knows by the power of the Spirit when and where the hour of 'revolutionary' love-inspired engagement and when and where the hour of pro-existent endurance or of contemplative 'lostness' has come." Inherent in the temporary, preparatory nature of earthly existence is the fact "that the Church and the Christians must keep themselves open to both duties".[2]

Readiness is everything: readiness for engage-

[2] K. Lehmann, ed., *Theologie der Befreiung* (Einsiedeln: Johannes Verlag, 1977), 71–72.

ment with Christ for God's concerns in the world, whether this engagement be a meaningful, active endeavor to further among mankind Christ's principles and his solidarity with the poor and oppressed, or an endurance—not to be simply called passive, since it is, again, active in a different way—in order to cooperate, together with the Crucified, in transforming souls, that is, in their process of purification toward a valid witness. This Christian readiness in both directions, toward action as well as endurance, can be meaningful and total. Precisely this constitutes its superiority over that other great readiness for engagement in our times, namely communism, to which suffering, the monstrous, humanly unaccountable phenomenon of suffering, counts for nothing except to be overcome. But does it, by even the slightest chance, look as though they will overcome it or even as though the person who no longer knows suffering were more human than the one purified by suffering? Even Nietzsche will convince us of the contrary.

Having said so much about martyrdom, we now have little space in which to add something about mission. Actually, it is not at all necessary to say something new. For the mystery of the rapid spread of Christianity in the first centuries, during which it was outlawed and often bitterly persecuted, is none other than that of the integral readiness of which we just spoke. In other words, it is a matter of absolute faith in him "who loved me and delivered himself up for me". This wondrous "for me", "for us", this *"admirabile commercium"*, this "marvelous exchange" between sin and grace on the Cross, gave Christian faith its superiority over every official or mystery religion and still gives it its personal power of attraction and its universal worth transcending all national boundaries. The fact of what happened to Jesus Christ was passed on without demythologizing question marks, just as the early Church and the Gospels witnessed to it. In this way, and only thus, did it possess its astonishing impact. Only in this way could it, as Paul says, be heard and effectively received for what it really was: God's word and not a human word (1 Th 2:13). The gospel that the Enlightenment of the seventeenth and eighteenth centuries has reduced to its merely human and moral components, or which the historico-critical scalpel of the nineteenth and twentieth centuries has truncated to isolated shreds that may possibly have originated with the historical Jesus, will scarcely be able to claim any missionary effect. The "enlightened" missionary simply tells persons of another faith or unbelievers what the latter already know as human beings:

that they ought to be good and neighborly in deed and thought. In the end, the "demythologized" missionary makes himself ridiculous when he tries to gain followers for a Christ of faith but must at the same time confess that he does not know whether the Jesus of Nazareth behind the believer's faith is really able to secure and justify it. Let us pay all due respect to historical criticism, including that applied to the New Testament texts: it can help us to see many things more clearly, in better perspective. But it is very quickly confronted with a decision, either to accept the uniform collective witness of the New Testament writings as it is meant—the early Church, so succesfully missionary, did just that—or to question this witness against the background of one's own kind of truth, to split it up into things that are reasonable to the so-called modern person and those which are no longer reasonable. As though the crucified Jesus as the final word of divine salvation for the world were reasonable to Jews and Gentiles of his time! No, he was certainly not that; and it was precisely because this proclamation produced such a shock and was so much counter to everything traditional that the primitive Christian mission was successful. For in this shocking fact lay once and for all the proof of God's love for the world that would have nothing to do with him, a love so foolish as to deliver up his only Son. The entire wisdom of ancient philosophy—of Celsus, Plotinus and Porphyry—was no match for this divine folly. And the real identity of this Jesus, who apparently expressed such foolishness, is attested by his words and deeds, his entire self-giving that is unparalleled among all the sages and founders of religion. Wherever one leaves everything together—the historical Jesus and the resurrected Christ, the Synoptics, Paul and John—there the true image of Jesus rises resplendent, and behind it the image of God, really plastic, three-dimensional, stereoscopic and so concrete that its truth and its claims are immediately evident.

Is it still evident today? Or must mission change its methods of proclamation or even discontinue its entire activity? The answer is not hard to find. For the plastic picture of Jesus to shine before people's eyes, the witness to Jesus—in Greek, his *martys*—must be plastic himself and his existence tangibly three-dimensional. He cannot present God's unreserved love with personal reservations. He must *live* his sending—in Latin, his *missio*. As Kierkegaard says, he has to gesticulate with his whole existence. Naturally he is not to do so in such a way that people will look at him as they would at a trapeze artist, but only so that his message becomes credible. With this condition fulfilled, *one* witness to the faith who genuinely lives his mission can accomplish more than a hundred professional missionaries routinely pursuing their trade. But of course, all this is a banal foregone conclusion for us Christians, because all of us have more or less experienced the truth of these things. *One* Christian, priest or lay person, in whom we have experienced the truth of Christian witness has more lastingly impressed us than scores of nominal Christians who could also be called something else, if need be, without changing radically. And *one* priest who has fundamentally disappointed a young soul, because this person had hoped to encounter a witness and found something completely different, can have a life on his conscience.

"Where life grows cold, law looms large" (G. Simmel). Where living witness to Jesus Christ no longer radiates from Christians, the machinery attempting to keep the domestic and foreign missions going increases. This machinery is not useless where it promotes a lively exchange between the homeland and the mission territory, especially where it keeps the native Christian vitally aware that he himself is not in the hinterland but, like all Christians, is permanently at the front, in the foremost firing line, where it is a matter of life or death. Péguy has expressed this with incomparable force and beauty, and I know no better way to conclude this consideration than with the words of this great Christian.

> [The Middle Ages] is spoken of as an age of faith. This is correct, if in saying it one means that for centuries—for centuries of Christianity, of the commandment of love, of the reign of grace— faith in the accepted truth was something held in common, literally something public, running in the community's blood and veins, living in the people, not only finding assent but being lived in a solemn, official way, whereas this is no longer the case today. *Historically* this is correct. At the same time, however, the great question remains un- answered as to whether our fidelity today, our Christian faith today, immersed as it is in modern culture and passing inviolate through the modern world, through the few centuries that constitute modern times, has not thereby acquired a rare beauty, a beauty as yet unknown, a unique grandeur in God's eyes. It is not ours to judge. But even if we leave the saints out of the picture, including the modern saints living in our time, we sinners too, without becoming proud, should see things as they are. I mean that our perseverance, our modern faith, attacked as it is from all sides, oppressed, isolated in this modern world, in the billows of an entire world, incessantly lashed by the foam and

storm, yet upright, isolated in this world, upright in an inexhaustibly raging surf, lonely on the ocean, inviolate, intact, in no way shaken or fissured or undermined, in the end still forms a beautiful memorial before the face of God.

To God's glory.

Who does not ultimately see that this Church and Christianity of our day, as Christian immersion in the modern world, as Christian travelling through modern times, possesses a kind of great, singular, tragic beauty, much like the great beauty, not exactly of a widow, but of a woman who has to guard a stronghold alone—one of those tragic ladies of the castle who for years on end had to keep the fortress intact for her lord and master and husband. Who does not see that our fidelity in the faith is more than the feudal fidelity of old, that our standing firm, our faith, our fidelity possess a countenance of their own, till now unknown, because they have undergone challenges unheard-of till now?

Our fidelity is somehow more faithful than the fidelity of old. Our faith is more than ever a faith that endures. Today every Christian is a soldier. There are no more complacent Christians. The Crusades that our ancestors pursued into infidel lands come to us of themselves today. We have them in our own homeland. Our fidelity in the faith is a citadel. The Crusades that shifted whole peoples, casting one continent on another, have swept back on us, penetrating into our dwellings. The infidels, individually or collectively, subtly or tangibly, formlessly or well-defined, invading everything, sanctioned by public law—and still more the infidelities, the perfidies—have brought the battlefield right to our doorstep. The lowliest among us is a soldier. The least among us is literally a crusader. All our homes are fortresses on the sea.

This means, then, that the virtues formerly required of a certain fraction of Christianity are demanded today of the whole of Christianity. A battle or ordeal that was formerly the object of a special vow, and therefore voluntary, is in our times required, and thus demanded. It is dictatorially imposed, without and even before our being able to take a stand on it: without our being asked. Without our having to express our opinion about it. In this regard, the jest applies: everyone is a soldier despite his free will.

What a mark of confidence in the troops! Among us Christians there is literally compulsory military service. It is a general draft. We are so much counted on that where others were free we are compelled. What was offered to our ancestors is imposed on us. They themselves had to "take up the Cross" and set out for elsewhere. In our case, God gives us the Cross (what a mark of confidence!) for an unceasing crusade right where we are. We are all at the front.

In summary, we can conclude from the poet's words that witness, *martyrion*, is less a matter of dying than of living at each moment. A death for Christ is only the terminal situation of a daily struggle to live for Christ under the motto "onward with vigorous fighting", urged on by Paul's reflection: "Since one died [out of love] for all, then [actually] all died. And he died for all so that the living may no longer live for themselves but for him who died for them and was raised" (2 Cor 5:14–15).

Then as now, this was martyrdom and mission.